... Chinese Games With Dice And Dominoes...

Stewart Culin

Nabu Public Domain Reprints:

You are holding a reproduction of an original work published before 1923 that is in the public domain in the United States of America, and possibly other countries. You may freely copy and distribute this work as no entity (individual or corporate) has a copyright on the body of the work. This book may contain prior copyright references, and library stamps (as most of these works were scanned from library copies). These have been scanned and retained as part of the historical artifact.

This book may have occasional imperfections such as missing or blurred pages, poor pictures, errant marks, etc. that were either part of the original artifact, or were introduced by the scanning process. We believe this work is culturally important, and despite the imperfections, have elected to bring it back into print as part of our continuing commitment to the preservation of printed works worldwide. We appreciate your understanding of the imperfections in the preservation process, and hope you enjoy this valuable book.

SMITHSONIAN INSTITUTION.
UNITED STATES NATIONAL MUSEUM.

CHINESE GAMES WITH DICE AND DOMINOES.

BY

STEWART CULIN,

Director of the Museum of Archæology and Palæontology, University of Pennsylvania.

From the Report of the U. S. National Museum for 1893, pages 489-537, with plates 1-12, and figures 1-33.

WASHINGTON:
GOVERNMENT PRINTING OFFICE.
1895.

(RECAP) (~~ANNEX B2~~)
4288
.277
.2

CHINESE GAMES WITH DICE AND DOMINOES.

BY

STEWART CULIN,

*Director of the Museum of Archæology and Palæontology,
University of Pennsylvania.*

CHINESE GAMES WITH DICE AND DOMINOES.

By Stewart Culin.

"The earth hath bubbles, as the water has, and these are of them."

This paper,* of which a preliminary study was printed in 1889,† is the first of a series on Chinese games, to be continued by similar accounts of playing cards and chess. It has been considerably extended, through recent studies in connection especially with the collection gathered by the author in the Anthropological Building in Chicago, and that in the National Museum.‡

The games described are chiefly those of the Chinese laborers in America, a limitation found as acceptable as it is necessary, since even among these people, who all came from a comparatively small area, there exist variations in the methods of gambling, as well as in the terminology of their games. The latter is made up largely of slang and colloquial words and presents many difficulties. The gamblers are usually men of the most ignorant class, and those most familiar with the games are often the least able to furnish correct Chinese transcriptions of the terms employed in them, so that the task of interpretation would have been extremely difficult but for the assistance received from Chinese and Japanese scholars.§

---

* This paper has been prepared at the request of the authorities of the U. S. National Museum, to illustrate a portion of its extensive collection of games.

† Chinese Games with Dice. | By Stewart Culin.—Read before The Oriental Club of Philadelphia. | March 14, 1889. | Philadelphia. | 1889. 8°. pp. 1-21.

‡ This collection, though the author modestly refrains from mentioning the fact, owes much of its completeness to Mr. Culin's own generous contributions.

G. Brown Goode.

§ The Chinese words printed in italics are transliterated according to Dr. Williams' "Tonic Dictionary of the Chinese Language in the Canton Dialect," Canton, 1856. Dr. Hepburn's Japanese-English Dictionary has been followed for Japanese, and the Korean words, in the absence of any native standard of orthography, and for the purpose of convenient reference, have been made to accord with that admirable work, the *Dictionnaire Coréen-Français*, Yokohama, 1880.

492   REPORT OF NATIONAL MUSEUM, 1893.

GAMES WITH DICE.

Chinese dice* are small cubes of bone marked on each side with incised spots from 1 to 6 in number, (fig. 1) which are arranged in the same manner as the spots on modern European dice, as well as those of Greece and Rome of classical antiquity;† the "six" and "one," "five" and "two," and "four" and "three" being on opposite sides.

The "four" and "one" spots on Chinese dice are painted red, and the "six," "five," "three," and "two" are painted black. The "one" is always much larger and more deeply incised than the other spots, possibly to compensate for its opposite, the "six."

Fig. 1.
CHINESE DICE.

The origin of the custom of painting the "fours" red is accounted for, according to the *Wa Kan san sai dzu e*,‡ by the following story:

> An emperor of the Ming dynasty (A. D. 1368–1643) played at *sugoroku* with his queen. He was almost defeated by her, but had one way of winning through the dice turning "fours." He cried and threw the dice, and they came as he desired, whereupon he was exceedingly glad, and ordered that the "fours" thereafter be painted red, in remembrance of his winning.

A similar story was related to me as a common tradition among the Cantonese, by an intelligent Chinese, who gave the emperor's name as *Lò Ling Wong*,§ who reigned under the title of *Chung Tsung* (A. D.

---

* The common name for dice among the Cantonese is *shik tsz'*, composed of *shik*, "colors," and *tsz'*, "seed," "dice."

In Medhurst's English and Chinese Dictionary, Shanghai, 1847, three other names for dice are given: *t'au tsz'* composed of *t'au*, written with a character compounded of the radicals, *kwat*, "bone," and *shü*, "a weapon," "to strike," and the auxiliary *tsz'*; *shéung luk*, "double sixes," from what is regarded as the highest throw with 2 dice, and *luk ch'ik*, literally "six carnation." The last name may be considered as a compound of the terms for the most important throws: "six" and carnation or red; the "four," to which, as will be seen, an especial significance is attached, as well as the "one," the lowest throw with a die, being painted red. In Japanese dice are called *sai*, a word written with a Chinese character, *ts'oi*, "variegated," "lucky."

† About the only dotted cubical dice which depart from this arrangement are those of the ancient Etruscans, which are regarded as having the "one" and the "three," "two" and "four," and "five" and "six" opposite, a system which does not appear, according to the writer's observation, to have been constant.

‡ "Japanese Chinese Three Powers' (Heaven, Earth, Man) picture collection." Osaka, 1714; vol. 17, fol. 4.

§ Whence a vulgar name for dice among the Cantonese, *hot lò*, composed of *hot*, "to call out loud," and *lò*, for *Lò Ling Wong*.

Modern Indian dice are usually marked with black and red spots. In the Mâhâbhârata (IV, 1, 25) reference is made to "dice, dotted black and red." (Prof. E. W. Hopkins, J. A. O. S., vol. 13, p. 123.)

684, 701–710). Mr. Herbert A. Giles* tells me that this story is mentioned by a Chinese author, but I am inclined to regard the account as fanciful, and think that it is probable that the color of the "fours" was derived, with the dice themselves, from India.

Several sizes of dice are used by the Chinese, varying from a cube of two-tenths to one of seven-tenths of an inch. Different sizes are employed in different games, according to custom.

Dice are usually thrown by hand into a porcelain bowl, the players throwing around in turn from right to left, and accompanying their efforts with cries of *loi!* "come!"

The Chinese laborers in the United States play several games with dice, but they are not a popular mode of gambling, and are generally neglected for *fán t'án*, and Chinese dominoes.

SZ' 'NG LUK.

The best known of these games is called *sz' 'ng luk*, "four, five, six," commonly contracted to *sing luk*, and is played with 3 dice of the largest size. The throws in it in the order of their rank are: "Three alike from three "sixes" down, called *wai*.† "Four, five, six," called *sing luk* or *chün fá*.‡ Two alike, the odd die counting from "six" down to ace, the last throw being called *yat fat*, "ace negative." One, two, three, called *mò lung*, "dancing dragon," or *shé tsai*, "little snake."

The first player is determined, on throwing around, to be the one who throws the highest number of red spots. The other players lay their wagers, usually in sums divisible by 3, before them. The first player throws until he makes one of the above mentioned casts. If he throws *sing luk* ("four, five, six"); 3 alike; or 2 alike, "six" high, each of the players at once pay him the full amount of their stakes; but if he throws *mò lung* or *yat fat*, he pays them the full amount of their stakes. If he throws 2 alike, "five," "four," "three," or "two" high, the next player on his left throws. If the latter makes a higher cast, the first player must pay him, but if a lower cast, he must pay the first player. The amounts thus paid are usually proportionate to the difference between the throws with the odd die. If it is 4 or 3, the full amount; if 2, two-thirds, or if 1, one-third of the stakes must be paid.

The third player throws in the same way, and the game is continued until the first player is out-thrown.

---

* Chinese dice are the exact counterpart of our own except that the ace and four are colored red; the ace because the combination of black and white would be unlucky and the "four" because this number once turned up in response to the call of an Emperor of the T'ang dynasty, who particularly wanted a "four" to win him the *partie*. (Strange stories from a Chinese Studio, Vol. II, p. 145.)

† *Wai* means "to inclose," and is a term that is also employed in Chinese games of chess and cards.

‡ Literally, "strung flowers."

KON MÍN YÉUNG.

Kon mín yéung, "pursuing sheep," is played with 6 dice of the largest size. It is a game played for small stakes, usually for something to eat, and is seldom resorted to by professional gamblers.

In it the player throws until he gets 3 alike, when the sum of the spots on the other dice is counted.

The throws in the order of their rank are: Six "sixes," called *tái mín yéung*, "large sheep." Six "fives," "fours," "threes," "twos," or "ones," called *mín yéung kung*, "rams." Three alike and "six, six, five," called *mín yéung ná*, "ewes." Three alike and the other throws than the above. These are designated by the number representing the sum of the throws with the 3 odd dice.

The throws, *tái mín yéung* and *mín yéung kung*, take all the stakes. If *mín yéung ná*, or any other cast of 3 alike, is made, the next player throws until he gets 3 alike, when he pays if his throw is lower, or is paid if it is higher, as in *sing luk*.

The throw of 3 "fours" is called *wong p'ang fúi*, concerning the origin of which name the following story is related:

A boy and girl were betrothed by their parents. The girl's father died, and the family having been reduced to poverty, her brother sold the girl to become a prostitute. This she resented, and anxious to find her betrothed, whose face she well remembered, she caused it to be advertised that she would yield herself to the man who could throw 3 "fours" with the dice. Many, attracted by her beauty, tried and failed, until her husband, Wong p'ang-fúi, who had obtained the rank of *kái ún*, or senior wrangler at the provincial examination, presented himself. For him she substituted loaded dice, with which he threw 3 "fours," whereupon she disclosed herself, and they were happily united.

CHÁK T'ÍN KAU.

Chák t'ín kau, "throwing heaven and nine," is played with 2 dice. In this game the 21 throws that can be made with 2 dice receive different names, and are divided into two series, or suits, called *man*, "civil," and *mò*, "military."

The 11 *man* throws, in the order of their rank, are figured on the right of Plate I. They are:

"Double six," called *t'ín*, "heaven."
"Double one," called *tí*, "earth."
"Double four," called *yan*, "man."
"One, three" called *wo*,* "harmony."
"Double five," called *múi*, "plum (flower)."†

---

*This throw is called by some *ngo*, a "goose," a name, like those of the throws that follow it in this series, evidently derived from a fancied resemblance of the spots on the dice.

†The 5 spot is also called by the name of *mume* or "plum (flower)," in Japan. In Korea the same name, *mai-hoa*, "plum flower," is given to the sequence "five, one;" "five, two;" "five, three;" "five, four;" "five, five;" "five, six" in the game of *Ho-hpai*, with dominoes.

REPORT OF NATIONAL MUSEUM, 1893.—CULIN. PLATE I.

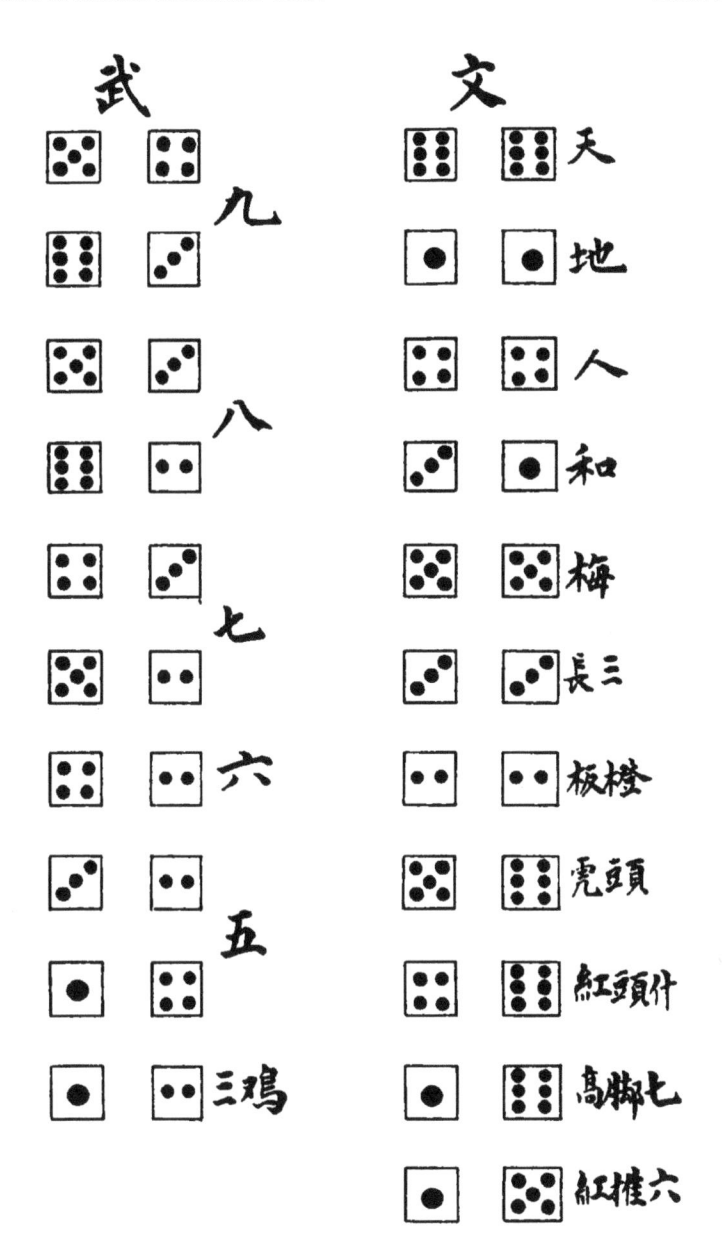

武　　　　　　文

九　天
　　地
八　人
　　和
　　梅
七　長三
　　板櫈
六　斃頭
　　紅頭仆
五　高脚七
　　紅摧六
三鷄

CHINESE DICE.

"Double three," called *ch'éung sám*, "long threes."
"Double two," called *pán táng*, "bench."
"Five, six," called *fú t'au*, "tiger's head."
"Four, six," called *hung t'au shap*, "red head ten."
"One, six," called *kò kéuk ts'at*, "long leg seven."
"One, five," called *hung ch'ui luk*, "red mallet six."

The 10 *mò* throws in the order of their rank are figured on the left of Plate I. They are:

"Five, four," and "six, three," called *kau*, "nines."
"Five, three," and "six, two," called *pát*, "eights."
"Five, two," and "four, three," called *ts'at*, "sevens."
"Four, two," called *luk*, "six."
"Three, two," and "four, one," called *'ng*, "fives."
"One, two," called *sám*, "three," or *sám kai*, "three final."

The first player determined, the other players lay their wagers on the table. The first player then throws and his cast determines the suit, whether *man* or *mò*, for that round. No other throws count and

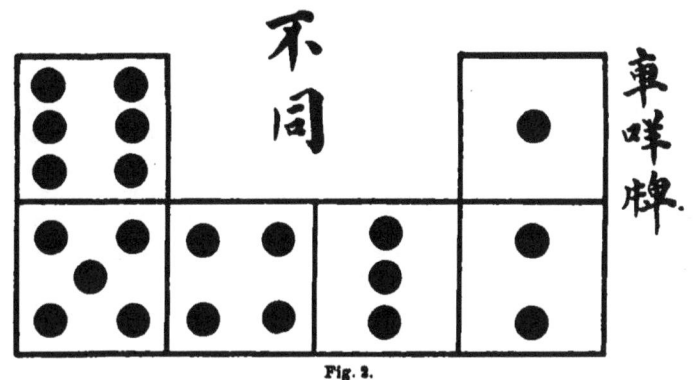

Fig. 2.
PÁT CHÁ BOARD: CHINA.

the players throw again, if necessary, until they make a cast of the suit led. If the first player throws the highest pair of either series, that is the "double six" of the *man*, or one of the "nines" of the *mò*, each player at once pays him, but if he leads the lowest of either suit, that is, the "five, one," or "one, two," he pays them the amount of their stakes.

If he throws any other pair than the highest or lowest of either suit the second player throws, and is paid his stakes, if he throws higher, by the first player, or pays him if he throws lower. The game is continued until the first player is outthrown, when he is succeeded by the second player, and the others lay their wagers as before.

PÁT CHÁ.

Pát chá, "grasping eight," is played with 8 dice, preferably of the smallest size. In this game the banker is provided with a diagram (fig. 2) numbered or dotted, like the 6 faces of a die, upon which the players place their stakes. It bears the legend *pat t'ung*, "unlike," which expresses the desire of the banker as to the manner in which the dice shall fall. A player throws 8 dice. If at least 3 fall like the number bet on, the gamekeeper pays him 8 times, or if 6 or more are like the number bet on, 16 times the amount of his stakes. In any other event, the player loses. A similarly marked tablet is used in playing with the *ch'é mé*, or teetotum (fig. 3). This implement is made with 6 dotted sides. The players lay their stakes upon the numbers on the tablet, and win 4 times the amount of their stakes if the one played on turns uppermost, or lose, if another number comes up. The *ch'é mé* is said to have its sides decorated sometimes with pictures of fish and animals instead of numbers or spots, and the diagram, which is called the *ch'é mé p'di*, or the "tablet for the teetotum," is then similarly inscribed (fig. 3).[*]

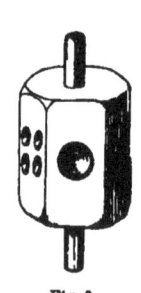

Fig. 3.
CHINESE TEETOTUM.
(From specimen in the museum of the University of Pennsylvania.)

CHONG ÜN CH'AU.

Chong ün ch'au is a game played with tallies, *ch'au*, the highest of which is called *chong ün*, the name given the *Optimus* at the examinations for the degree of Hanlin, whence I have styled it "The Game of the Chief of the Literati." (pl. 3.) Two or more persons may play, using 6 dice and 63 bamboo tallies. The latter receive the following names:

First. One piece about 6 inches in length, called *chong ün*, the first of the Hanlin doctors. This counts as 32.

Second. Two shorter pieces called *pong ngán*, second of the Hanlin, *t' ám fá*, third of the Hanlin. Each count as 16.

Third. Four shorter pieces called *úi ün*, the First of the *tsun sz'*, or literary graduates of the third degree. Each count as 8.

Fourth. Eight shorter pieces called *tsun zs'*, literary graduates of the third degree. Each count as 4.

---

[*] A similar game from Manila, Philippine Islands, in the United States National Museum (Plate 2), consists of a cardboard with 6 equal divisions, with numbers, represented by disks of colored paper, from 1 to 6; a hexagon-shaped top with numbers from 1 to 6, and a saucer in which to spin it. It is described by the collector, Hon. Alex. R. Webb, United States Consul, under the name of *prinola*, as a popular game in the market places with the native women. "Bets are placed on the spots on the board, the top is spun rapidly in the saucer, and the winners are paid double the amount of their bets. Only one number can win, of course the one corresponding to that which turns up when the top stops turning, and the chances are therefore quite largely in favor of the dealer." The name is evidently the Portuguese *pirinola*, but the game is probably of Chinese or Indian origin. In India a 6-sided teetotum, *chukree*, identical with the Chinese, is used, and is turned like a top on a wooden or china plate. "The stakes are placed on a board with 6 partitions, and the game is decided on the settling of the die with a particular number uppermost. The play of this game is allowed only during the Diwali festival, when gambling is sanctioned as a religious observance." (Ms. catalogue of Indian games and toys procured for the Chicago exhibition. Provincial Museum, Lucknow, India.)

Report of National Museum, 1893—Culin.

PLATE 2.

THE GAME OF PRINOLA.
Cat. No. 154184, U. S. N. M. Manila, Philippine Islands.

TALLIES FOR "CHONG ÜN CHAU."
Cat. No. 153905, U. S. N. M. Kwangtung, China.

Fifth. Sixteen shorter pieces called *kü yan*, graduates of the second degree. Each count as 2.

Sixth. Thirty-two shorter pieces called *sau ts'oi*, graduates of the first degree. Each count as 1.

The first, second, and third classes bear rude pictures and names, but the others are usually distinguished only by their size.

Two or more persons can play. The players throw in turn from right to left, and after throwing each draws the tallies he is entitled to according to the appended table. If the tally called for by a throw has been drawn, its value may be made up from the remaining ones; but the winner of the *chong ün* must surrender it without compensation if another player makes a higher throw than that by which he won it. The one who counts highest becomes the winner.

The game is said to be played by women and children, and is not played by the Chinese laborers in the eastern United States, although they are generally acquainted with it.

A set of implements for this game from Johore in the collection of His Highness the Sultan at the Columbian Exposition was similar to that above described, and was evidently of Chinese workmanship. It was catalogued under the name *chong wan chiam* (*chong ün ch'au*), the tallies being called *buah-buah bertulis*.

The throws in *chong ün ch'au*, in the order of their rank, are:

| 6 "fours." | 6 "fives." | 6 "twos." |
| 6 "sixes." | 6 "threes." | 6 "ones." |

These throws are called *ts'un shik*, and take all the tallies:

5 "fours" and 1 "six," or 1 "five," or 1 "three," or 1 "two," or 1 "one."
5 "sixes" and 1 "four," or 1 "five," or 1 "three," or 1 "two," or 1 "one."
5 "fives" and 1 "four," or 1 "six," or 1 "three," or 1 "two," or 1 "one."
5 "threes" and 1 "four," or 1 "six," or 1 "five," or 1 "two," or 1 "one."
5 "twos" and 1 "four," or 1 "six," or 1 "five," or 1 "three," or 1 "one."
5 "ones" and 1 "four," or 1 "six," or 1 "five," or 1 "three," or 1 "two."
4 "fours" and 1 "three" and 1 "one."
4 "fours" and 1 "twos."
4 "sixes" and 1 "four" and 1 "two."
4 "sixes" and 1 "five" and 1 "one."
4 "sixes" and 2 "threes."
4 "fives" and 1 "four" and 1 "one."
4 "fives" and 1 "three" and 1 "two."
4 "threes" and 1 "two" and 1 "one."
4 "twos" and 2 "ones."
4 "fours" and 2 "sixes."
4 "fours" and 1 "six" and 1 "five."
4 "fours" and 2 "fives."
4 "fours" and 1 "six" and 1 "three," or 1 "six" and 1 "two."
4 "fours" and 1 "five" and 1 "three," or 1 "six" and 1 "two."
4 "fours" and 1 "five" and 1 "two," or 1 "five" and 1 "one."
4 "fours" and 2 "threes," or 1 "three" and 1 "two."
4 "fours" and 1 "two" and 1 "one," or 2 "ones."

Each of the above throws counts as thirty-two, and takes the *chong ün*.

H. Mis. 184, pt. 2——32

2 "fours," 2 "fives," and 2 "sixes."
2 "ones," 2 "twos," and 2 "threes."
3 "fours" and 3 "sixes," or "fives," or "threes," or "twos," or "ones."
3 "sixes" and 3 "fives," or "threes," or "twos," or "ones."
3 "fives" and 3 "threes," or "twos," or "ones."
3 "threes" and 3 "twos" or "ones."
A sequence from "one" to "six."

Each count as 16, and takes either the *pong ngán* or *t'ám fú*. Three "fours" with any combination except those mentioned count as 8, and take one of the *úi ün*. Four "sixes," 4 "fives," 4 "threes," 4 "twos," or 4 "ones," with any combination of 2 dice except those already mentioned count as 4, and take one of the *tsun sz'*. Two "fours" count as 2 and take one of the *kü yan*. One "four" counts as 1, and takes one of the *sau ts'oi*.

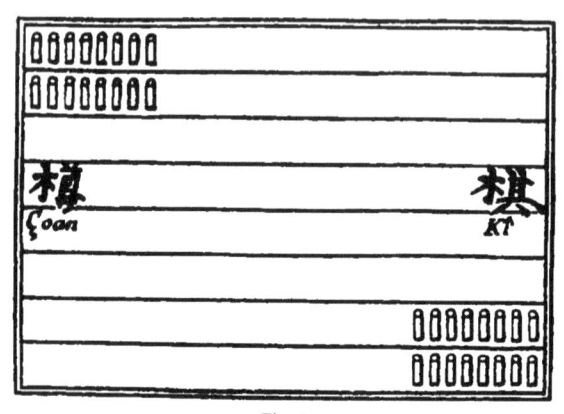

Fig. 4.
CHINESE BACKGAMMON.
(From De Ludis Orientalibus. 1694.)

The Chinese game similar to backgammon, which that accomplished scholar, Dr. Thomas Hyde, described in his work on Oriental games under the name of Chinensium Nerdiludium (The Nerd Game of the Chinese)* is not played by the Chinese laborers in America, nor do any I have met appear to be acquainted with it (fig. 4.)

According to Dr. Hyde, it is called by Chinese *Çoan Ki*, which he translates as *erectus ludus*, or *erectorum ludus*, but which might be rendered as "the bottle game" or "bottle chess" *Çoan* (*tsun*), meaning a vase or bottle, and *Ki* (*k'i*) being a generic name for games played with men as chess.

This game is played with dice and small upright pillars, from which the name is derived. The board is divided into eight equal parts by transverse lines, and the pieces, which are from 2 to 3 inches high and number 16 on each side, are arranged upon it when the playing commences, as seen in the figure.

The pieces are moved line by line, according to the throws with the dice, from the places on the left to the eighth place on the right, and from thence ascending to the

---

* De Ludis Orientalibus. Oxford, 1694, p. 65.

opposite side and back to the starting place, the player who first gets all his pieces there winning the game.

Two dice are thrown, and the pieces are moved to the places which the number of the throws directs. One may move whatever piece or pieces one chooses, according to the number, either pieces which have been moved before or those which have not yet been moved. If, instead of upright pieces, one plays with small flat discs, which is also permitted, they may be placed side by side or piled on top of each other, as seems most convenient.

A throw of 2 "ones" causes a piece to be set aside and delivered up as lost, or, if the game is played for money, it loses the player the tenth part of his stakes. Whoever throws "twos" or "threes" begins moving to the second or third lines, and so on. If doublets are thrown, one may move to the place corresponding to the half number of such doublets; and this may be done by moving 1 piece once to such half number, or 2 pieces at the same time to the place corresponding with such whole number, for in this case either 1 or 2 pieces together may be moved. If "five" and "six," which make 11, are thrown, one may move 1 piece to the fifth place and another to the eleventh, or else move 2 pieces at the same time to the tenth line or place, and then 1 of them to the next line, which is the eleventh. And thus with respect to other throws: If single (as "two" and "four"), for the single numbers move as many places, but if joined (as "five" and "six"), then otherwise, as already stated.

The game of backgammon, played upon a board of 24 stations similar to the boards in common use in Spain at the present day, exists along the entire eastern coast of Asia, from Korea to the Malay Peninsula.

SSANG-RYOUK.

In Korea the game of backgammon is known as ssang-ryouk (Chinese *shéung luk*), double sixes. It is played with wooden pins or men (fig. 5), called *mal* (Chinese *má*), "horses," upon a hollowed board, *ssang-ryouk-hpan*[*] according to the throws with two dice.

The throws receive the following names:

 1-1, *syo-syo* (Chinese *sú sú*), "smallest."
 1-2, *tjout-kko* (Chinese *shü pí*), "rat nose."
 1-3, *syo sam* (Chinese *sú sám*), "small and three."
 1-4, *pdik sd* (Chinese *pdk sz'*), "white and four."
 1-5, *pdik s* (Chinese *pdk 'ng*), "white and five."
 1-6. *pdik ryouk* (Chinese *pdk luk*), "white and six."
 2-2, *tjoun-a* (Chinese *tsun á*), "superior two."

---

[*] *Hpan*, the word used for "board" in *ssang-ryouk*, as well as Korean chess and other Korean games, is written with the Chinese character meaning "an order," "rank," which the Cantonese call *kuk*. The men are about 3¼ inches in height. Fifteen are employed on each side, one set being painted red and the other left the natural color of the wood. They are usually made of boxwood, but some softer wood is employed for the cheaper sets.

Dice are called in Korean *tjyou-sd-á* (Chinese *chü shd*, "vermillion," *á?*), and are identical in every respect with those of China. The only other Korean games with dice than *ssang-ryouk* with which I am acquainted are as follows: One which my informant tells me has no particular name, but which might be called *tjyou-sa-á-nol-ki*. Three or four boys sit around, and one puts a peanut or pine nut on the floor and the die is thrown, the nut going to the one throwing the highest. The other, consists in the substitution of a cubical die for the four staves used in the prevailing Korean game of *nyout-nol-ki*.

2-3, *a sam* (Chinese *á sám*), "two and three."
2-4, *a sd* (Chinese *á sz'*), "two and four."
2-5, *koan-a* (Chinese *kún d*), "sovereign two."
2-6, *a ryouk* (Chinese *á luk*), "two and six."
3-3, *tjyang-sam* (Chinese *ch'éung sám*), "long three."
3-4, *sam sd* (Chinese *sám sz'*), "three and four."
3-5, *sam o* (Chinese *sám 'ng*), "three and five."
3-6, *sam ryouk* (Chinese *sám luk*), "three and six."
4-4, *tjoun-hong* (Chinese *tsun hung*), "superior red."
4-5, *sd o* (Chinese *sz' 'ng*), "four and five."
4-6, *sd ryouk* (Chinese *sz' luk*), "four and six."
5-5, *tjoun-o* (Chinese *tsun 'ng*), "superior five."
5-6, *o ryouk* (Chinese *'ng luk*), "five and six."
6-6, *tjoun-ryouk* (Chinese *tsun luk*) "superior six."

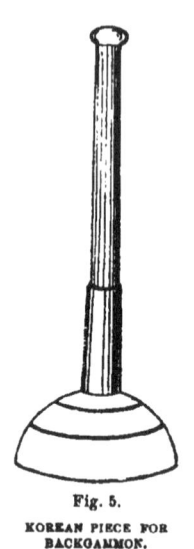

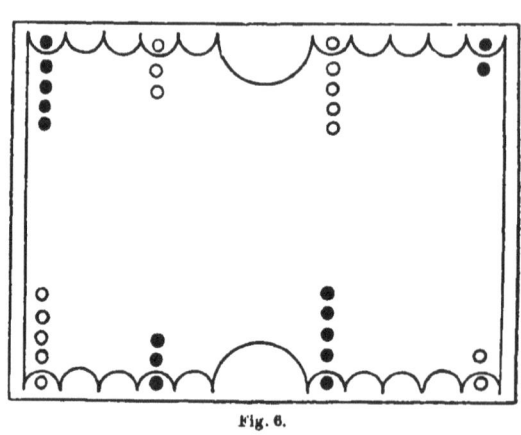

Fig. 5.
KOREAN PIECE FOR BACKGAMMON.

Fig. 6.
SSANG-RYOUK (BACKGAMMON) BOARD: KOREA.

A diagram of the board, set as at the commencement of the game, is shown in fig. 6.

The board has mortised sides, which extend about 2 inches above the surface. The divisions on either side, called *pat* (Chinese *t' ín*, "fields"), are simply outlined in black. The larger ones in the middle are not counted in moving, and are used to throw the dice in. The first player is determined by the highest throw with 1 die. The pieces are moved around according to the throws, as in the English game of backgammon; but it is customary to move 2 pieces when doublets are thrown, and doublets do not entitle the player to another throw, nor to any additional count than if the dice were dissimilar.

A player may take an opponent's piece, which must be again entered, as in the English game. This is called *tjap-ta*, "to catch." When a player gets all his men around into his home place he bears them off according to his subsequent throws.

SAKA.

In Siam the game of backgammon is known as *saka*, and is played upon a board, represented in fig. 7, with 2 dice.* Sixteen discs of ivory,

Fig. 7.
SAKA (BACKGAMMON) BOARD: SIAM.

like draftsmen, are used on each side, one set being white and the other, red. The small compartments on either side of the board are

Fig. 8.
KRABOK, CYLINDER FROM WHICH DICE ARE THROWN.
(Siamese Backgammon.)

said to be intended for cowries (*bia*), which are used as counters. The pieces are entered, according to the throws, in the right-hand side of the board opposite the player, and are moved around, as in our game, to the side directly opposite, where they are thrown off. A player does not take his opponent's pieces. The dice are not thrown directly with the hand, but are loaded into a tube (*krabok*) of ivory, about 3 inches in length (fig. 8), called *krabok saka*, and shot obliquely through another cylinder of ivory, 2½ inches high (fig. 9), called by the same name, placed upon the board. These implements correspond with the Roman *fritillus* or dicebox, and the *pyrgus*, the latter being defined as "a little wooden tower on the side of a gaming board, hollow,

Fig. 9.
CYLINDER INTO WHICH DICE ARE THROWN.
(Siamese Backgammon.)

and having steps inside, through which the dice were thrown upon the board.†

---

* Dice are called in Siamese *lok bat*. They are identical with those of China.
† Andrews's Latin-English Lexicon.

TABAL.

A backgammon board from Johore, exhibited by His Highness the Sultan in the collection of games at the Columbian Exposition under the name of *tabal*, is represented in fig. 10. It is played with 2 dice, *dadu*, those exhibited being marked in black and red, like those of

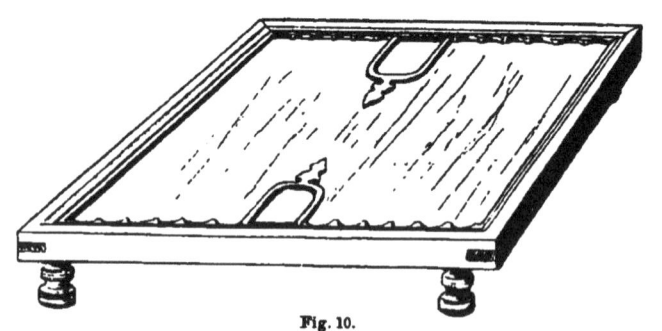

Fig. 10.
TABAL (BACKGAMMON) BOARD: JOHORE, MALAY PENINSULA.
(From specimen in the Museum of the University of Pennsylvania.)

China. The name of the game, *tabal*, is doubtless from the Portuguese *tabola* or Spanish *tabla*, and *dadu* from the Portuguese or Spanish *dado*, "a die."

SUGOROKU.

The game described by Dr. Hyde agrees in some respects with the Japanese game of *sugoroku*, as illustrated in native encyclopedias. In fig. 11, reproduced from the *Kum mō dzu e tais ei*,[*] the board is

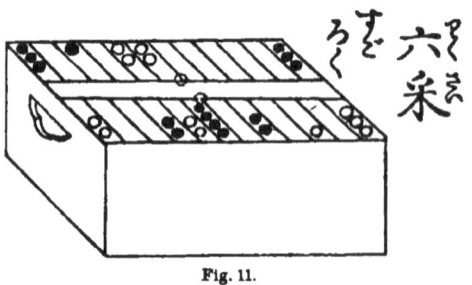

Fig. 11.
SUGOROKU BOARD: JAPAN.

represented as being divided into 12 parts by longitudinal lines, which are broken in the middle by an open space similar to the *ho kái*, or "dividing river," of the Chinese chessboard. According to the same work the 12 compartments, called in Japanese *me*, or "eyes," symbolize the 12 months, and the black and white stones, with which the game is played, day and night.

---

[*] "Very Complete Collection of Pictures to Teach the Unenlightened." Kiyoto, 1789, vol. 4, part 8, fol. 5.

The moves are made according to the throws of the dice, the name being derived from that of the highest throw, *sugoroku* (Chinese, *shéung luk*), or "double sixes."*

Sugoroku appears to be of great antiquity in Japan. The *Wa Kan san sai* states that it is recorded in the Japanese Annals that *sugoroku* was forbidden in the time of Jitō Tennō (A. D. 687–692), and that it is probable that it was played in Japan before the game of *go*† was brought to that country. The same encyclopedia, in the careful manner usual in such works, makes a number of citations from Chinese authors with reference to the origin of the game. It says it is recorded in the Suh sz' ch'ï‡ that Ts'ao Chih§ of Wei invented *sugoroku*, and used 2 dice for it, but at the end of the Tang dynasty (A. D. 618–913), the number of dice was increased to 6.

It is written in the Wú tsáh tsú that *sugoroku* is a game that was originally played in Hú (Japanese, *Ko*), the country of the Tartars. It relates that the King of Hú had a brother who was put to death for a crime. While in prison he made the game of *sugoroku* and sent it to his father, writing with it a few words in order to make known how men are oppressed by others when they are single and weak.

The Ngán lui yáu states that *sugoroku* came from the T'ien Chuh, "India."

The name of *sugoroku* is applied at the present day in Japan to various games played upon boards or diagrams, in which the moves are made by throwing dice.‖ Of these there are many kinds, among

---

* *Sugoroku* is also called *rokusai*, as will be seen from the names appended to fig. 11.

† Chess, by which the game of 360 men, half black and half white, called by the Chinese *wai k'í* is meant.

‡ I am unable to identify either this or the two following works quoted in the *Wa Kan san sai*.

§ Ts'ao Chih (A. D. 192–232) was the third son of the great usurper, Ts'au Ts'au, who overthrew the Han dynasty. He was distinguished by precocious talent and poetical genius, and devoted himself wholly to literary diversions. (The Chinese Reader's Manual, No. 759.)

‖ The name is also applied to at least one simple dice game in which no board or diagram is used. Mr. Kajiwara informs me that in the Province of Aomori, a common game with 2 dice is called *ichi-san sugoroku;* so called from the name of the highest throw, *ichi san*, "one, three."

Japanese dice at the present day usually have their 6 faces marked with black dots. Those used by gamblers are said to be larger than the kind employed in popular amusements. The dice games are said to vary in different parts of the Empire. Japanese sailors in New York City play a game with 2 dice called *chō han*, "even and odd." They throw 2 dice under a cup. The even throws are called *chō* and the odd *han*. The players, two or more in number, bet on the even or odd by calling out and laying their wagers before them while the cup remains inverted over the dice. They use foreign playing cards cut lengthwise in strips and tied in bundles of 10 as counters, instead of money; a custom that they say has its origin in the use of the narrow Japanese playing cards, or bamboo tallies at home for this purpose. The same game, under the same name, called by the Chinese *chéung pun*, is known to the Cantonese laborers in the United States as a common game in China.

which the most popular is called *dō chiu*, or "traveling" *sugoroku*. It is played upon a large sheet of paper, on which are represented the various stopping places upon a journey; as, for example, the 53 post stations between Tokio and Kiyoto, and resembles the games of "snake" and "steeplechase," familiar to English and American children.* Such games are much played by the Japanese at the season of the the New Year, when new ones are usually published. In 1889, Japanese newspapers reported that two new games of *sugoroku* found much favor in Tokio.

Fig. 12.
JAPANESE CHILDREN PLAYING SUGOROKU.

The same general name would be given by the Japanese to the following Chinese game, which I have occasionally seen played by the clerks in Chinese stores in our cities.

SHING KÚN T'O.

Shing kún t'o, the "table of the promotion of the officials," is the celebrated game which is best known through Dr. Hyde's account as "the game of the promotion of Mandarins."†

It is played by two or more persons upon a large paper diagram, on which are printed the titles of the different officials and dignitaries of the Chinese Government. The movements are made by throwing dice, and the players, whose positions upon the diagram are indicated by notched or colored splints, are advanced or set back, according to their throws.‡

The following story was related to me concerning the invention of the game:

---

*A paper diagram for a game of *sugoroku* is entitled, according to the characters on the sheet, *Hokkaidō shin dō ichi ran sugoroku*, or "A glance at the Hokkaidō new road *sugoroku*." This game was published in 1873 on the occasion of the opening of a new road through the southern part of the island of Yesso, from Hakodate to Sapporo, the capital.

The diagram consists of an impression in colors, 32½ by 20 inches, and is divided into 38 parts, exclusive of the goal and starting place. These contain pictures of the scenery at the different stations on the road, each division having a tablet beside it on which the name of the place is written, with the distance to the next stopping place. The game is played with 1 die, the players throwing in turn, and advancing from the lower right-hand corner to the goal at the center. Each spot of the throw counts as one station on the diagram. If a player's move leaves him upon a division having the character *tomare*, "stop over," he loses his next throw. When a player near the goal makes a higher throw than is just necessary to take him to the central space, he is set back; if he has an excess of 1, to the fifth place from the goal; 2, to the fourth place, and so on.

† De Ludis Orientalibus, p. 70.

‡ A similar but much simpler game, with the titles of Japanese instead of Chinese officials, is played in Japan under the name of *kwanroku*.

CHINESE GAMES WITH DICE AND DOMINOES. 505

The Emperor Kienlung (A. D. 1736-1796) was in the habit of walking at nightfall among the houses occupied by the candidates for the degree of Hanlin, who came up to Peking for the triennial examination; and hearing, night after night, the song of the dice issuing from one of them, he summoned the offender before him to explain his conduct. In excuse, fearing punishment, he told the Emperor that he had constructed a chart, on which were written the names of all the official positions in the Government, and that he and his friends threw dice, and according to their throws traversed the board, and were thus impressed with a knowledge of the various ranks and steps leading to official advancement. The Emperor commanded him to bring the chart for his inspection. That night the unfortunate graduate, whose excuse was a fiction created at the moment, sat until daybreak, pencil in hand, and made a chart according to his story, which he carried to the Emperor. That august prince professed to be much pleased with the diligence of the scholar who improved his mind, even while amusing himself, and dismissed him with many commendations.

This familiar sounding story can not be accepted without question, especially since it will be seen that Dr. Hyde published his account many years before the period mentioned; but my informant, a clerk in a Chinese shop in Philadelphia, may not have stated the date correctly.

The paper charts for the game may be purchased at the Chinese stores in New York and San Francisco. The names of the different offices are arranged upon them in rectangular divisions, alongside of each of which is a tablet with the name of the board or class under which those within it are included. They ascend from the lowest to the highest in successive stages, arranged in order around the chart from right to left, and from the outer division, which is devoted to provincial officials, to the innermost, which has the titles of the members of the metropolitan administration. The center is occupied with rules for playing.

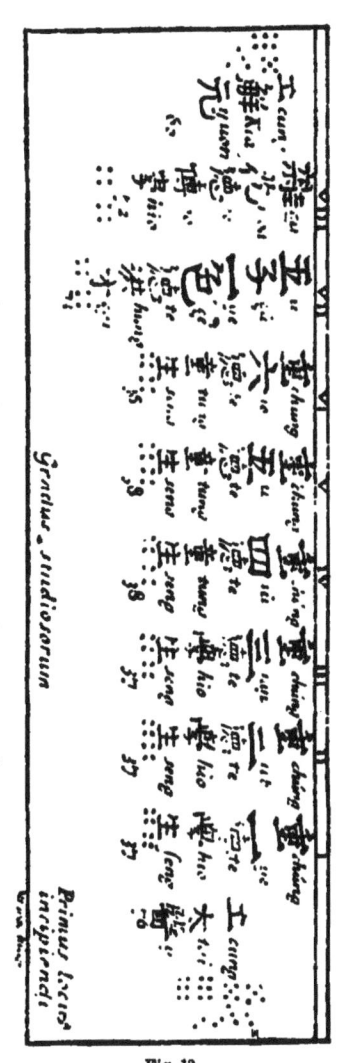

Fig. 13.
FIRST PLACES FOR ENTERING IN THE GAME OF "PROMOTION OF MANDARINS."
(From De Ludis Orientalibus, 1694.)

Four dice are thrown in turn by each player, instead of 6, as formerly recorded by Dr. Hyde. Entrance is obtained by making a cast, either of 4 alike, by which the player is at once advanced to an "hereditary rank;" of "three, four, five, six," called *ch'ün fá*; of 3 alike or 2 alike. All of these throws, in descending order, enable the player to enter one of the positions from which advancement may be obtained. Subsequent promotion depends upon the throws, doublets enabling the player to move once; 3 alike, twice; and 4 alike, 3 times. "Double fours" count highest, "double sixes" next, and so on down to "ones," through which the player is set back. The appropriate move for each throw is indicated in small characters beneath each of the titles on the chart.

A curious contrast is presented between the little sheet reproduced by Dr. Hyde (fig. 13), upon which only the principal officials of the Ming dynasty are represented, and that now current, whereon may be seen the innumerable ramifications of the Chinese "civil service" under the present Tartar domination.

The charts such as I have seen used in the United States are printed in Canton, and bear an impression about 23 inches square. They are divided into 63 compartments, exclusive of the central one and the place for entering at the lower right-hand corner. The latter contains the names of 13 different starting places from *yan shang*, or "honorary licentiate," down to *t'ung shang*, or "student," between which are included the positions of *t'in man shang*, "astrologer," and *i shang*, "physician." These are entered at the commencement of the game by the throws of "three, four, five, six," 3 "fours," 3 "sixes," 3 "fives," 3 "threes," 3 "twos," and 3 "ones;" and then in the same manner double "fours," and so on down to double "ones."

The 63 compartments, representing as many classes of officials or degrees of rank, comprise 397 separate titles, of which the highest, and the highest goal of the game, is that of *man fá tín tái hok sz'*, or "grand secretary." This, however, under favorable conditions, can only be reached by a player who starts from a favorable point, advancement in the game being regulated by rules similar to those which actually regulate promotion under the Government. Thus a player whose fortune it is to enter as a physician or astrologer can only obtain promotion in the line of his service, and must be content with a minor goal, as he is ineligible to the high civil office of "grand secretary."

The dice are thrown into a bowl placed in the center of the sheet, the players throwing in turn, and each continuing to throw until he has made a cast of doublets or higher. It is noticeable that "fours," as in Dr. Hyde's account, constitute the highest throw. A pair of "fours," according to the rules, is to be reckoned as *tak*, "virtue," and leads to a higher place than those of other numbers. "Sixes" are next highest, and are to be reckoned as *ts'oi*, "genius;" and in the same manner, in descending degree, "fives" are to be reckoned as *kung*, "skill;" "threes" as *léung*, "forethought;" "twos" as *yau*, "tractability;" and "ones," *chong*, "stupidity."

The game is much complicated by being played for money or counters, which is necessary under the rules. By this means advancement may be purchased, degradation compounded for, and the winner of a high position rewarded.

The main point of difference in the game as it exists to-day and as described by Dr. Hyde is in the number of dice employed. The enlarged form of the diagram is of minor importance, as he himself says that the names of the officials written on the tablet are many or few, according to the pleasure of the players.

The game of *shing kún t'o* and the Japanese game of many stations, described under the name of *sugoroku*, I regard as having been derived from the ancient Tartar game played with staves, which exists at the

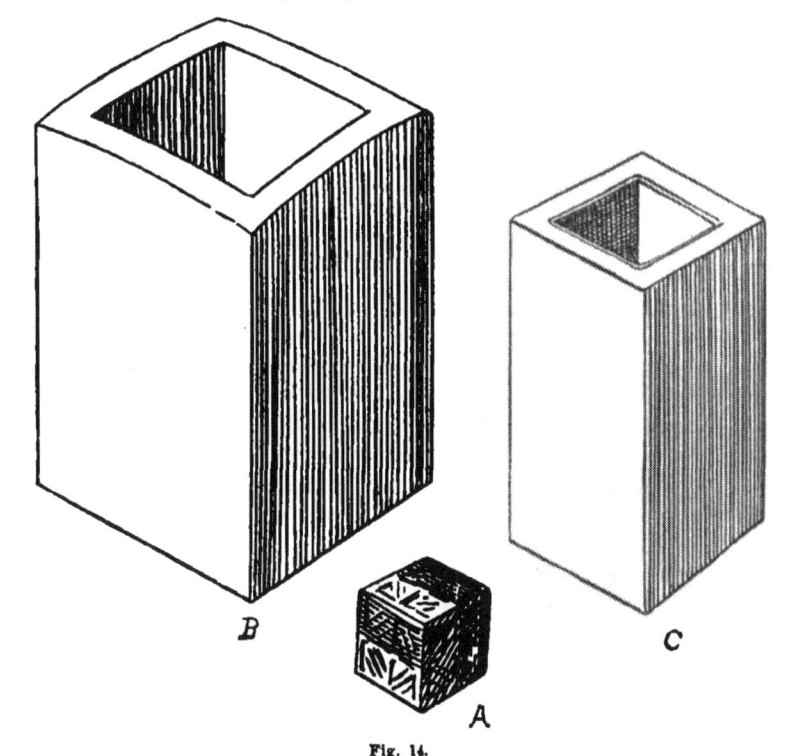

Fig. 14.
PÒ TSZ' (CHINESE).
(From specimen in the Museum of the University of Pennsylvania.)

present day in Korea under the name of *nyout-nol-ki*. As to the backgammon game, which I consider to be a development of the same game, and which I have described as existing in Korea, China, Japan, Siam, and the Malay Peninsula, I am uncertain whether it is indigenous, has come over from India, or been acquired from the Portuguese or Spaniards in the fifteenth or sixteenth century.

PÒ TSZ'.

The *pò tsz'*, or covered die, is not, properly, a die at all. It consists of a small wooden cube (fig. 14 a), which is placed in a square receptacle in the top of a brass prism (fig. 14 c), over which a brass cover (fig. 14 b) fits very closely. A specimen exhibited by His Highness, the Sultan of Johore in the section of games at the Columbian Exposition consisted of a wooden cube about one-half an inch square, having one-half of each face painted red and one-half white. The prism in which the cube fitted was slightly convex on the bottom, and, when placed upon a smooth surface, could be twirled rapidly. The game is played by placing the box containing the pò in the center of a square crossed by diagonal lines, which is drawn upon a mat. One of the four divisions of the square is painted red. The players lay their bets upon the other divisions, and the box is spun rapidly by the gamekeeper, who repeats the operation until it comes to rest squarely with the corners corresponding with the intersecting lines. The cover is then lifted, and those who have staked opposite the red side of the die win. The banker wins when the red side comes opposite the side of the square painted red.* There is said to be a current notion, amounting to a superstition among the Chinese in Johore, that if a player stops the box as it is spinning the luck will surely go against him.

KONG POH.

Another specimen in the Sultan's collection, called at Johore, *kong poh* (Chinese *t'ung pò*), "current treasure," furnishes an explanation of the name *pò*. It consists of a wooden die (fig. 15 a), with a face 1¾ inches square, and three-fourths inch thick, which fits into a brass box with a broad base (fig. 15 b). A wooden cover (fig. 15 c) fits over the box. This die is not spun, but is concealed in a bag which accompanies it, and there adjusted by the gamekeeper. The face of the wooden die is carved with the characters *t'ung pò* (fig. 15 d), on one side in the ordinary, and on the reverse in seal characters, the character *t'ung* being painted red, and *pò* white. The inscription *t'ung pò*, "current treasure," occurs on the face of all modern Chinese coins (fig. 15 d), and the common name of the game is evidently derived from the character *pò*, which occurs on this block.

GAMES WITH DOMINOES.[†]

Chinese dominoes, commonly called *kwat p'ái*,[‡] "bone tablets," consist of 32 rectangular pieces of wood, bone, or ivory, similar to those used in Europe and America (pl. 4).

They differ, in the absence of the "blank" in the Chinese series (fig.

---

* The Manners and Customs of the Chinese of the Straits Settlements, Singapore, 1879, p. 63. The Chinese laborers in the United States are generally unfamiliar with the game.

† Read in part before The Numismatic and Antiquarian Society of Philadelphia, November 4, 1886.

‡ This is the common name among the Cantonese. Medhurst's English and Chinese Dictionary, Shanghai, 1847, gives in addition two other names—*ngd p'ái*, "ivory tablets," and *tim tss' p'ái*, "dotted tablets."

Report of National Museum, 1893.—Culin. PLATE 4.

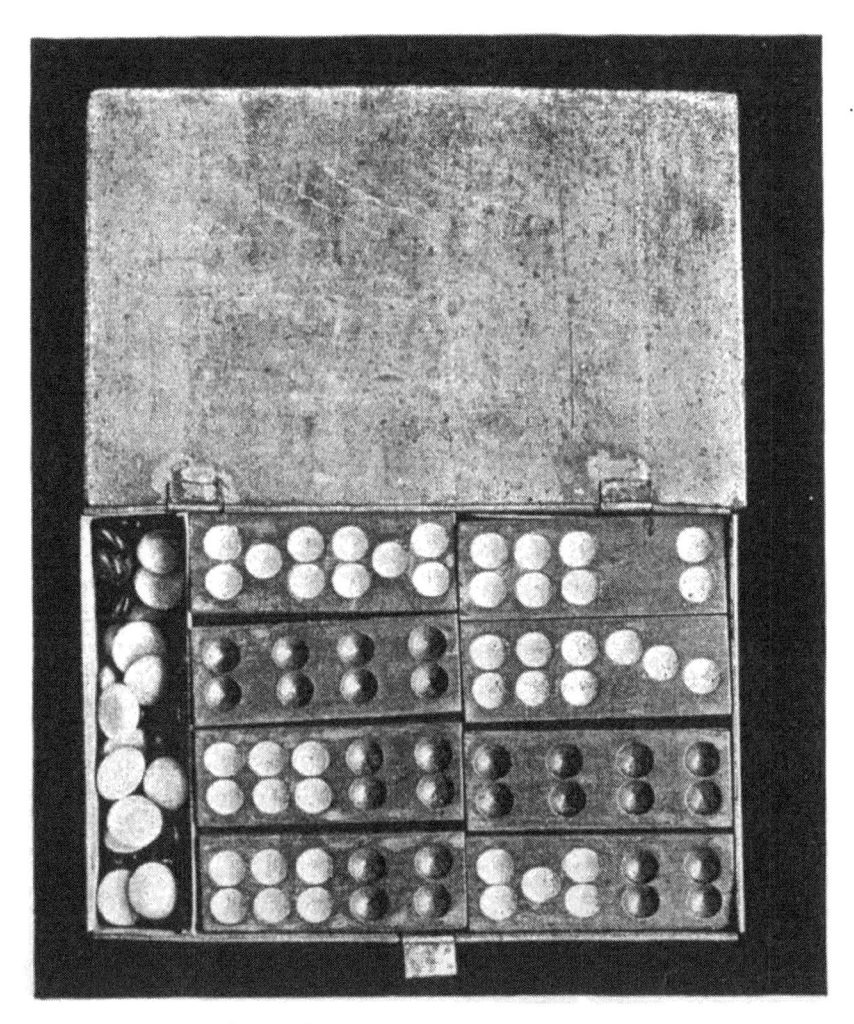

CHINESE DOMINOES WITH COUNTERS, IN TIN BOX.
Cat. No. 168908, U. S. N. M. Kwangtung, China.

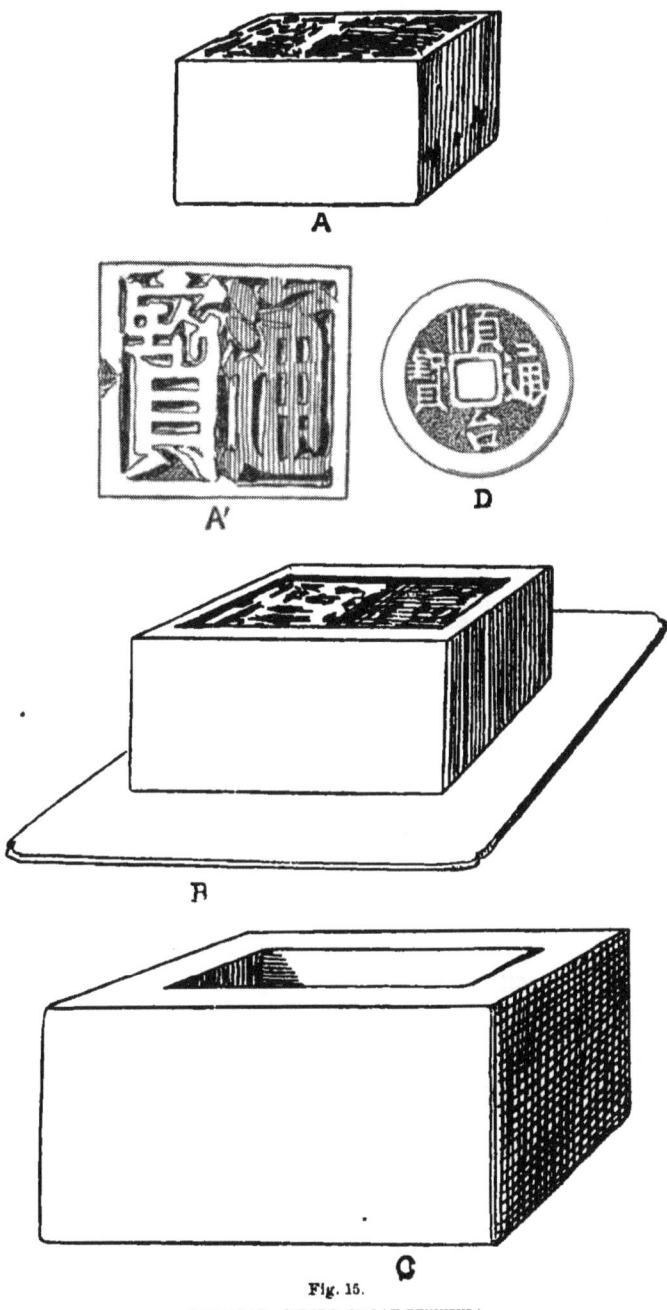

Fig. 15.
KONG POH. JOHORE, MALAY PENINSULA.
(From specimen in the Museum of the University of Pennsylvania.)

16), which commences with "double one" instead of "double blank," and contains 21 different pieces instead of 28 as in the European game (fig. 17). Eleven of the 21 pieces are duplicated, making 32 pieces in a set.

The "one" and "four" marks and the alternate "threes," which com-

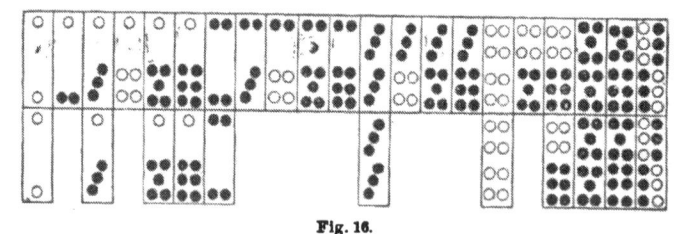

Fig. 16.
CHINESE GAME OF DOMINOES.

prise the "sixes," are usually painted red, while the other marks are painted black or white, depending upon the material of the dominoes.

The dominoes in common use in the Province of Kwangtung and among the Chinese in the United States are made of Chinese ebony

Fig. 17.
EUROPEAN GAME OF DOMINOES.

and are about 2⅜ inches long, seven-eighths of an inch in width, and three-eighths of an inch in thickness, with incised spots, which are painted red and white. The ends of each piece are usually ornamented with a single incised red spot, while the backs are sometimes uniformly marked with three spots, one red between two white, arranged diagonally across (fig. 18).

Fig. 18.
CHINESE DOMINOES: PROVINCE OF KWANGTUNG AND UNITED STATES.

The following Chinese games are those of the Chinese laborers in the United States, among whom they are the commonest gambling implements. They call each piece by name, and in certain games pair them according to the arrangements shown in plate 5. The 11 pieces that

Report of National Museum, 1893.—Culin. PLATE 5.

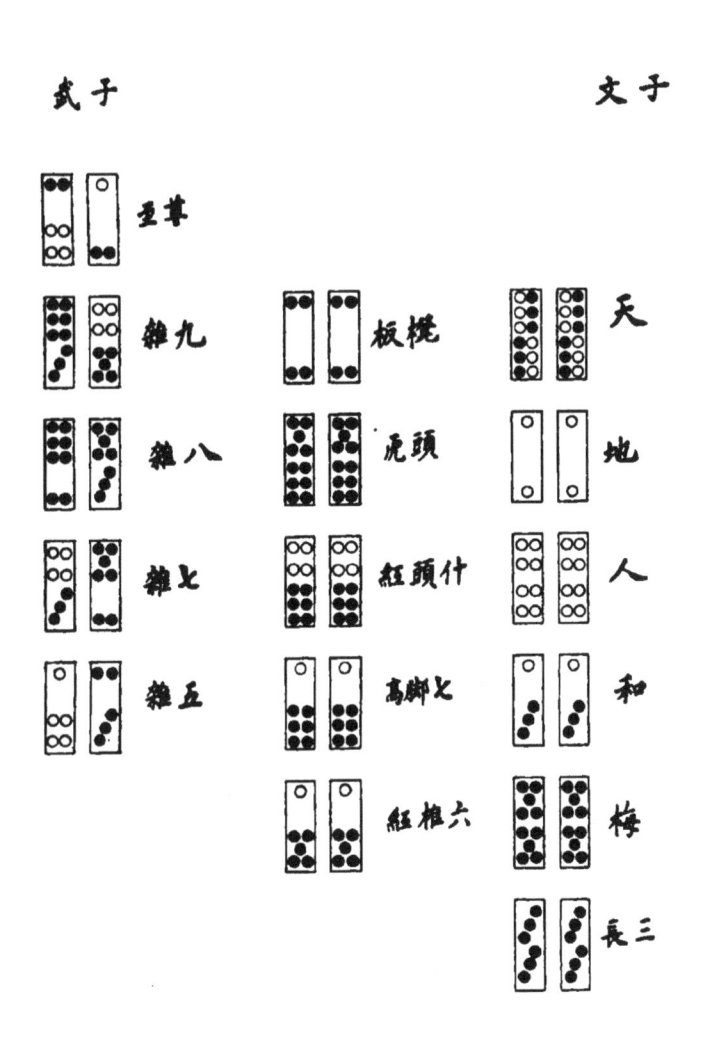

METHOD OF PAIRING CHINESE DOMINOES

are duplicated are paired with their doubles, and form a series or suite, to which they give the name of *man*, "civil," while the remaining 10 pieces are paired with each other, in accordance with the sum of their spots, and from a suite called *mò*, "military."

The *man* pieces, in the order of their rank, are:

6-6, called *t'ín*, "heaven."
1-1, called *tí*, "earth."
4-4, called *yan*, "man."
1-3, called *wo*, "harmony."
5-5, called *múi*, "plum" (flower).
3-3, called *ch'éung sám*, "long three."
2-2, called *pán tang*, "bench."
5-6, called *fú t'au*, "tiger's head."
4-6, called *hung t'au shap*, "red head ten."
1-6, called *kò kéuk ts'at*, "long leg seven."
1-5, called *hung ch'ui luk*, "red mallet six."

The *mò* pieces are:

2-4 and 1-2, called *chí tsün*, "supreme."
6-3 and 4-5, called *tsáp kau*, "heterogeneous nines."
6-2 and 5-3, called *tsáp pat*, "heterogeneous eights."
4-3 and 5-2, called *tsáp ts'at*, "heterogeneous sevens."
1-4 and 2-3, called *tsáp 'ng' luk* "heterogeneous sixes."

Both pieces in all the pairs are of equal value and rank in their suits

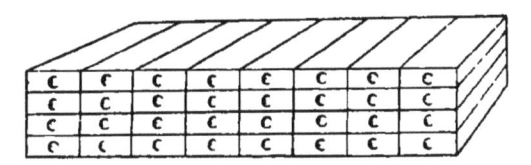

Fig. 19.
STACK OF DOMINOES AT OPENING OF GAMES.

in the order given, except those which compose the pair called *chí tsün*, which together form the highest pair, but separately are the lowest of the *mò* series.

The arrangement of the dominoes called *shéung tung*, or "stack," at the opening of games, is shown in fig. 19.

TIÚ Ü.

A simple game called *tiú ü*, "to angle," is played by 2 or 3 persons with 2 sets of dominoes. The pieces are well mixed and piled face down, side by side, in a stack 4 high. Four piles of 4 each are now drawn from one end of the stack and placed face up on the table. When 2 play, both players draw 3 piles (12 dominoes), or if 3 play, 2 piles (8 dominoes) from the same end of the stack. The players then examine their pieces, and the first player endeavors to mate one of his pieces with one having the same number of spots among those turned up on the table. If successful, he places the mated pair, face up, before him. In either case he draws the bottom piece of the pile at the end of the stack from which the last piles were drawn and endeavors to mate it with one of those on the table. If successful, he takes the pair, but if not, he places the piece drawn among those on the table. The second player then tries to mate one of his pieces, and also draws one from the stack, and the game is continued in this manner until the stack is exhausted. A pair of double "sixes" in a player's hand is at once laid out. If a player holds a piece in his hand, identical with 2 pieces on the table, and the fourth piece of the same kind has not been played, he may, at his turn, pile the 3 pieces that are alike one upon the other, with the uppermost face up, at the opposite end of the stack to that drawn from, and the player who first lays out the fourth piece may take the 3 pieces. The 2 pieces composing the *chí tsün* mate with each other, and form an exception in this game to the rule by which all pieces having the same number of spots mate with each other without reference to their belonging either to the *man* or *mò* series. When the last domino is drawn, the players examine those they have taken. The pieces on which the spots number 8 or more are called *tái ü*, "large fish," and count 2 points for each spot. The pieces below 8 are called *sai ü*, "small fish," and count 1 point for each red spot. If this latter sum is between 2 decades, the highest decade is counted. The player counting the highest becomes the winner, and is paid by each of the players for each point he has in excess.

TS'UNG SHAP.

Ts'ung shap, "to dispute for tens," is played by 2 persons with 1 set of dominoes. The pieces are piled face down, side by side, in a stack 4 pieces high, which the players divide between them, each player taking 8 of the 16 piles. The first player draws the top piece from the end pile towards the right of his pile, and lays it face up on the table. The second player, in turn, draws a piece and lays it face up alongside of the piece played by the first player. The players continue to draw and place the pieces on the table in this manner either on the right or left of the row thus formed. If a player lays down a piece which is a duplicate of one of the pieces at either end of the row, he takes both pieces, called *túi*, a "pair," and they count 10 for each spot on them at the end of the game. Or, if a player lays down a piece on which the spots, added to those on 2 pieces at one end of the row, or on the pieces at each end, form a sum that is a multiple of 10, the player takes the 3 pieces, and they count 1 for each spot on them at the end of the game. If there are but 2 pieces on the table, and a player takes them, he piles them upon each other to mark the play, called *táp tí*, literally "to tread on earth," i. e. a "sweep," which counts 40. The winner draws and lays out another piece. Should he fail to take up a winning combination of

2 or 3 pieces, his opponent may take it, and follow by laying out a piece and continuing the game. The game proceeds until one of the players has laid out all of his pieces, when the one who counts highest wins.

K'AP TÁI SHAP.

Kim tái shap, "to grasp many tens;" *Ch'i tái shap*, "to grasp many tens;" *K'ap tái shap*, "to complete many tens;" is played by any number of persons from 2 to 20 and upward, and is the favorite game with dominoes in the Chinese gambling houses in the United States. In many of these houses a large table covered with matting to deaden the sound is kept apart for this game. As there played, many sets of dominoes are used which are well mixed by the players and piled faces down, side by side, in piles 5 pieces high in a long stack upon the table. The croupier, or one of the players, shakes 4 dice under a cup, and counts around to the right, commencing with the player on his right, up to the number thrown. The one at whom he stops becomes the first player. The top piece on the third pile from one end of the stack, with each alternate piece on the top up to the number of persons playing, less-one, is now removed and placed in a pile at the other end of the stack. The first player takes 2 piles at the end and gets 10 pieces; the second player on his right takes the 2 next piles and gets 9 pieces, and so on, each player except the first getting 9 pieces.

In this game each piece in a set of dominoes may be mated with a duplicate piece to form a pair called *ngán*, "eye." The *ngán* or eyes thus formed by the pieces on the left (pl. 6) are called *ün ngán* or "weak eyes," while those formed by the pieces on the right are called *ngáng ngán*, or "strong eyes." The object of the game is to get 10 pieces in each of which 2 are the same and form either an *ün* or *ngáng ngán*, and the others form 4 pairs, in each of which the sum of the spots is 10 or a multiple of 10, whence the name of the game. The piece 2-4 is only counted as 3 in making up tens.

The players examine their pieces, and the first player if he has not drawn a winning hand, discards a piece which he throws face up on the table. The next player to the right may take this piece to complete a winning hand, or in exchange for a piece from his hand, which he places face up on the table. He also draws a piece from the bottom of the exposed pile of the stack. If it does not complete a winning hand he may either throw it face up on the table, or keep it and discard a piece from his hand. The third player may now take one of the pieces on the table and draw one from the bottom of the exposed pile. The game proceeds in this way until one of the players gets 10 pieces, of which 2 form a *ngán*, and the others pairs on which the sum of the spots is 10 or a multiple of 10 and wins the game.

In gambling houses the stakes are placed in a box on the table at the commencement of each game, the players all contributing the same amount. Five per cent is at once taken from the box for the gambling house, and the remainder goes to the successful player.

K'AP SHAP.

K'ap shap, "to complete tens;" *K'im shap*, "to grasp tens;" *Shap tsai*, "little tens." *K'ap shap* corresponds with the preceding game and is the name given to it when played by 2 persons. One set of dominoes are used and the pieces are arranged in a stack 4 high. The first player takes 8 and the second 7 pieces. The object of the game is to get 8 pieces, 2 of which form a *ngán*, or pair, and the others pairs on which the sum of the spots is 10 or a multiple of 10. In this game, as in *k'ap t'ái shap*, a winning hand is required to contain 1 *ngán*, or "eye." Slight variations from the manner here described occur in playing these games. The first player is frequently determined by drawing a domino and counting around, instead of by throwing dice.

NAÚ T'ÍN KAU.

Naú t'ín kau, literally "turning heavens and nines," from the names of the highest pieces of the 2 suits, is played by 2 persons. One set of dominoes are used, which are piled face down in a stack 4 high. The first player draws the top domino from the end of the stack toward his right, and the second player the one beneath it. The second player must draw a higher domino of the same suit, either *man* or *mò*, or the first player takes both pieces and places them on the table before him, with the face of the winning piece exposed on top. The winner continues drawing first until the other player draws a higher piece, when the latter takes both pieces and has the lead. The game is continued in this way until the stack is exhausted. Each of the players then counts the red spots on the exposed faces of the dominoes before him and the one having the highest total becomes the winner, and is paid for each red spot he has in excess by the loser.

TÁ T'ÍN KAU.

Tá t'ín kau, "to play heavens and nines," called, like the preceding game from the names of the highest pieces of the two suits, is the best and most highly developed of the Chinese games with dominoes. It is played by 4 persons with 1 set of dominoes. The 32 pieces are arranged face down in a stack 4 high to form 8 piles of 4 pieces each. One of the players throws 2 dice, and counts around to determine who shall be the first player. He is called *tsò chong*, "builder of the barn," or *chong ká*, and usually places some object on the table before him to indicate his position. A disk of wood inscribed with the character *chong* frequently accompanies sets of dominoes for this purpose. The first player takes 2 piles of dominoes. If the dice fall near one end of the stack of dominoes, the first player takes the 2 piles at that end,

Report of National Museum, 1893.—Culin. PLATE 6.

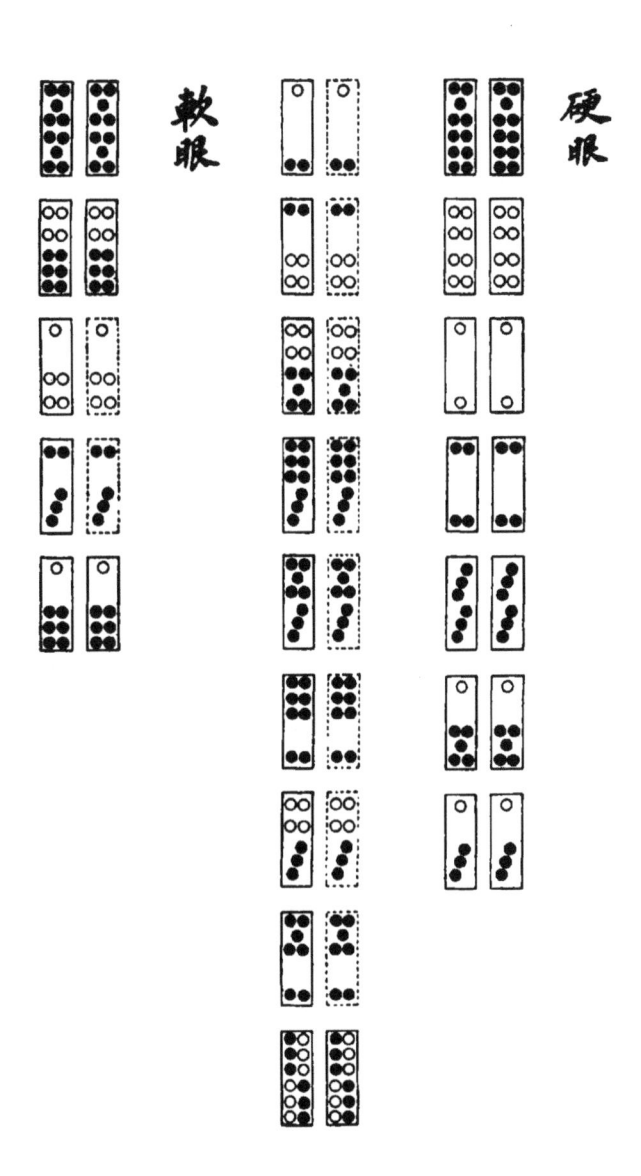

METHOD OF PAIRING CHINESE DOMINOES IN THE GAME OF KAP T'ÁI SHAP

the player on his right the next 2 piles; the third player to the right, the next two, and the fourth player the remaining rows. But if the dice fall near the middle of the stack, the first player takes the 2 middle rows; the player on his right the piles on the right and left of the middle ones, the third player the piles outside of these, and the fourth player the piles at the ends. The first player leads by placing 1, 2, 3, or 4 pieces face up on the table. One piece of either suit may be thus led, and a higher piece of the same suit will be required to take it; or a pair of either suit may be led, and a higher pair of the same suit will be required to take it; or one or both pieces of the first, second, third, or fourth pair of one suit (see pl. 5) may be led with one or both pieces of the corresponding pair of the other suit, and 2 3, or 4 pieces of corresponding higher pairs will be required to take them. That is, one or both of the 6-6 may be led with one or both of the pair 6-3, 4-5, and the pair of 1-1 with one or both of the pair 6-2, 5-3, and vice versa.

The other players follow from right to left, by playing as many pieces as are led, putting them on top of those on the table if they are higher, or beneath if they are lower than those already played. They are not required to follow suit. The winner leads again, and the game is continued until all the dominoes have been played. The player who takes the last round wins the game. He becomes the *tsò chong* for the next game. It is required of the winner, however, to take at least 2 tricks, so that if only 1 piece is led on the last round a player who has not won a trick is not allowed to take the trick, and the game goes to the next higher player. *Tá t'ín kau* is invariably played for money. A trick counts 1 point, for which any sum may be agreed upon. At the end of the game the players each pay the winner according to the number of tricks they have taken. The holder of 4 or more tricks pays nothing; of 2 tricks, for 2 points; of 1 trick, for 3 points, and a player who does not take a trick for 5 points. The first player, or *tsò chong*, however, always pays twice the amount when he loses, and is paid double when he wins, and so on throughout the game, paying and receiving in every case twice as much as the other players. Should the *tsò chong*, through winning the last round, hold his position over into the next game, his gains and losses are then in the ratio of 3 to 1 to those of the other players. In the third game they would be as 4 to 1, and so on.

If any player except the first player wins a round with the pair 2-4 1-2, called *chí tsün*, the first player must pay him 4 times, and the other players twice the sum agreed upon for 1 point; but if the first player takes a round with the *chí tsün*, the other players must pay him 4 times the value of a point.

If any player except the first takes a round with 4 pieces of 2 corresponding pairs, the first player pays him 8 times and the other players 4 times the value of a point, but if the first player takes the round the other players pay him 8 times the value of a point.

516   REPORT OF NATIONAL MUSEUM, 1893.

If a player takes 2 rounds with the *chí tsün* or 2 rounds with 2 corresponding pairs in 2 successive games, the amounts that must be paid him by the other players are doubled, and if he takes 3 such rounds in succession they are trebled. In gambling houses the winner of a round with the *chí tsün* must put the value of 1 point and the winner with 2 corresponding pairs of 2 points in a box for the house. This constitutes the only revenue derived by gambling houses from the game.

It is said that the custom of requiring the winner to take at least 2

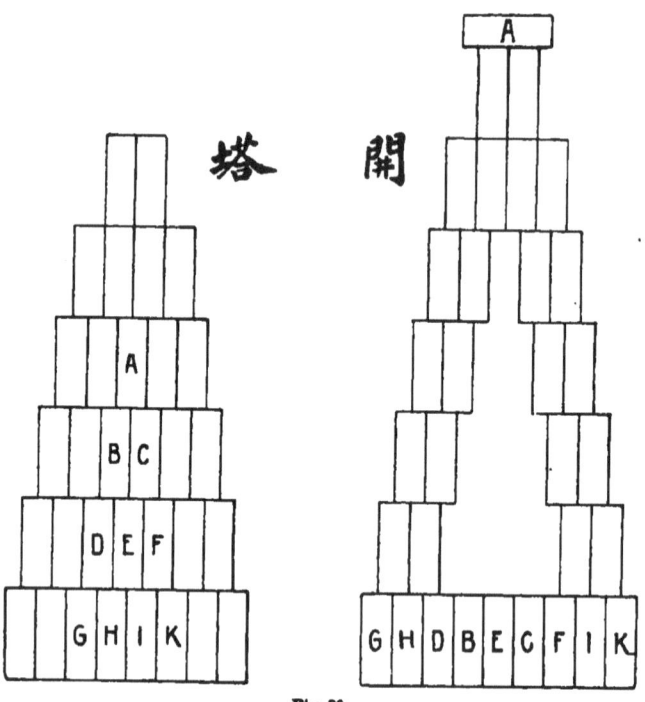

Fig. 20.
ARRANGEMENT OF DOMINOES IN GAME OF HOI T'ÁP.

tricks is an innovation of the last hundred years. Formerly the person taking the last trick became the winner, although it was the only trick taken by him during the game.

HOI T'ÁP.

Hoi t'áp, "to open the pagoda," is a game of solitaire played with dominoes. One set of dominoes are placed face down and arranged in the form of a pyramid, with 2 pieces at the apex and 4, 5, 6, 7, and 8, in the successive rows beneath, as shown in the diagram on the left of fig. 20.

The center domino, A, in the third row from the top, is then pushed down, taking with it the small pyramid composed of the pieces B, C of

Report of National Museum, 1893.—Culin. PLATE 7.

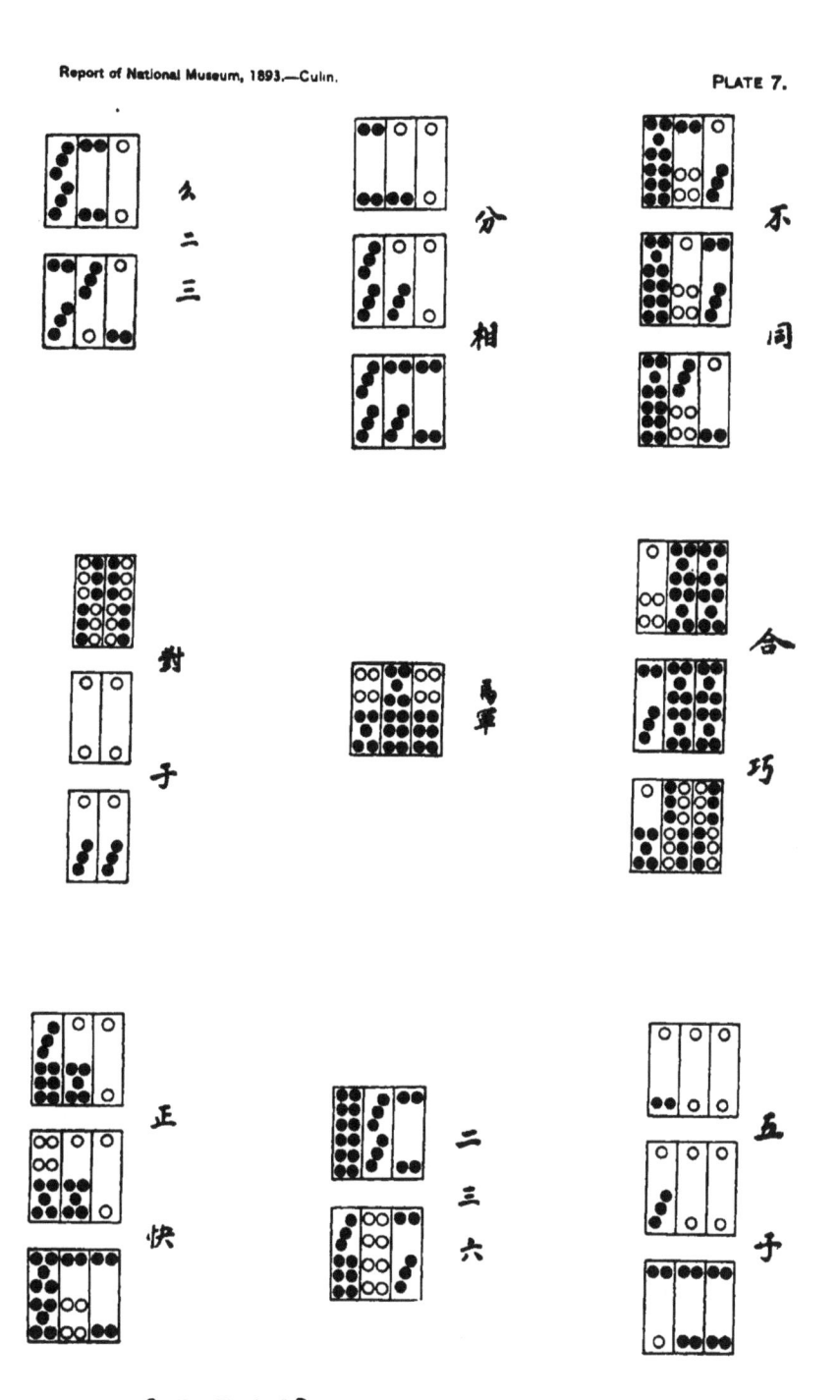

COMBINATIONS OF DOMINOES, SIGNIFICANT IN FORTUNE TELLING.

the fourth row, D, E, F of the fifth row, and G, H, I, K of the sixth row. The piece A is then placed transversely, face up, across the top of the original pyramid, and the other pieces that were withdrawn formed into a line, face up, at its base; the pairs G-H and I-K being put at the ends, D and F within them, B, C next within and E in the middle, as in the diagram on the right of fig. 20. The players then proceed to mate the pieces that are face up, according to the arrangement found on pl. 5. When no more pairs can be made with the exposed pieces the outside piece on the right of the second row from the top may be reversed. If it can not be paired it is left in its place, but if mated the outside piece on the third row is liberated, and may be reversed, and so on. When the right-hand side is blocked, the piece on the left of the second row may be reversed, and the same plan followed as before. When the piece A is mated the two pieces beneath it may be reversed; and the removal of the two pieces at the ends of the lowest row, as G H, permits the pieces directly above them to be reversed. The process is continued until the game is blocked, or the player has mated all the pieces comprising the pyramid.

This game is said to be used in divination, the success or failure in mating all the pieces being regarded as furnishing a clew to the determination of the event under consideration.

FORTUNE TELLING WITH DOMINOES.

Dominoes are regularly used in fortune telling in China at the present day, and their use for this purpose is generally known to the laborers who come to America. I have before me a book entitled *Ngá p'ái shan shò t'ò chü ts'éung kái*, "a chart for finding out the numbers by divine aid and with ivory dominoes, with an explanation and commentary." This work was printed in Canton in 1865, the name of the author being given as Ch'ing Ngok. The preface, which professes to explain the attributes and astrological significance of the dominoes, is followed by a series of diagrams illustrating different combinations formed with dominoes taken three, or in one class, two at a time. Specimens of the different classes are represented in pl. 7.

The following names and numerical values are given to them:

pat t'ung, "unlike," counts 6.
hòp káu, "ingeniously divided," counts 4.
'ng tsz', "five spots," counts 5.
fan shéung, "divided reciprocally," counts 3.
má kwan, "cavalry," counts 3.
í sám luk, "two, three, six," counts 3.
tsí í sám, "ace, two, three," counts 3.
tùi tsz', "corresponding spots," counts 3.
ching fái, "correctly satisfied," counts 1.

In telling fortunes an entire set of dominoes is placed face down upon a table and well mixed. The dominoes are then all placed side by side in a row and reversed. The manipulator selects from this row as many combinations as possible, formed by adjacent pieces, according to the diagrams, and adds together the numbers corresponding with them. This sum is referred to the following table and result noted:

1 to 4 is to be esteemed *hă hă*, "lowest"
5 to 7 is to be esteemed *chung hă*, "below the middle."
8 to 9 is to be esteemed *chung p'ing*, "even middle."
10 to 11 is to be esteemed *shéung shéung*, "highest."

The dominoes are then reversed again and mixed, and the preceding operations twice repeated, and 3 sets of terms from the above series obtained. Reference is then made to the text of the book. This consists of 125 pages, arranged in order under all the different combinations that may be formed with the 5 pairs of terms given above, taken 3 pairs at a time, commencing with *shéung shéung, shéung shéung, shéung shéung*. An oracular verse, apparently of original composition, is found on each page, referring to some well-known personage or incident, with a short text to aid the diviner in applying the prognostication to the various affairs of life.

DOMINOES FROM FUHCHAU.

Before proceeding to discuss the origin and antiquity of the Chinese game, an account will be given of dominoes used in other parts of China, and among the people of the adjacent countries.

A set of dominoes from Fuhchau[*] in the Oriental Section of the Museum of Archæology and Palæontology of the University of Pennsylvania is made of bamboo and numbers 32 pieces. They measure 1¾ by 1¾ by 1¾ inch, and have slightly curved faces that follow the natural curve of the reed. The concave faces are marked with incised spots that are painted red and green, and are arranged in the Chinese series (fig. 17), green taking the place of black spots. These dominoes are accompanied with 16 wooden disks resembling draughtsmen, an inch in diameter, the faces of which are reproduced in plate 8. They each bear a Chinese character referring to one of the 16 pairs formed with the 32 dominoes.[†] Four of these, *t'in, ti, yan,* and *wo,* are the same

---

[*] Received through the courtesy of J. P. Cowles, esq., U. S. vice-consul, Fuhchau.

[†] Prof. Rudolfo Lanciani, in the Athenæum, January 7, 1888, gave an account of the discovery of a tomb in Perugia twenty-one centuries old, in which an inveterate gambler had been buried together with his gambling apparatus. Among other remarkable sets were "16 *tesseræ*, or labels, cut in bone, 4 inches long, with a word engraved on one side and a number on the other." The importance of the discovery is concentrated on the words and numbers engraved on the bone labels. The ancients used to give a special name to a certain number, or addition of numbers, which they obtained by throwing the dice. * * * As regards the newly discovered labels, it appears that any number from 1 to 12 was considered a very bad throw, and consequently the corresponding words or names were very objectionable indeed (*Mœchus Vappa*, ect.). The "13" is neither good nor bad; hence its name, *vix rides*, "you hardly smile." The names corresponding to higher numbers are all of good omen, such as *benignus* (25), *amator* (30), and *felix* (60), which seems to be the maximum of the game discovered at Perugia." While the agreement of number of tablets in this Etruscan series with those in the Chinese is probably a mere coincidence, it is curious to note the occurrence of such similar usages in ages and countries so widely separated.

PLATE 8.

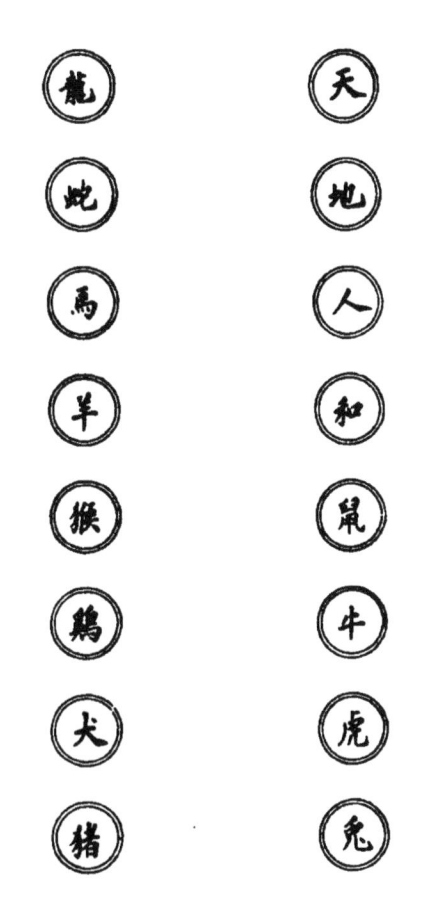

龍　天
蛇　地
馬　人
羊　和
猴　鼠
鷄　牛
犬　虎
豬　兔

FACES OF WOODEN DISCS ACCOMPANYING DOMINOES FROM FUHCHAU.
From specimens in the Museum of the University of Pennsylvania.

as those used to designate the four highest pieces in the *mán* series, plate 5, but the remainder, in place of the vulgar names usually given to the other pairs, have the characters *shü, ngau, fú, tô, lung, shé, má, yéung, hau, kai, hün,* and *chü,* which represent the names "rat," "ox," "tiger," "hare," "dragon," "serpent," "horse," "goat," "monkey," "cock," "dog," and "pig," the 12 animals of the duodenary cycle.* I understand these discs are used in connection with a kind of lottery.

I am informed that bamboo dominoes, similar to the above, are used at Shanghai, and at all the Chinese ports from Fuhchau northward.

There are several very interesting sets of Chinese dominoes from Fuhchau in the museum of the Long Island Historical Society, Brooklyn, N. Y.† One of these sets (A) consists of 126 marked pieces and 2 blanks. They are made of bamboo, faced with bone or ivory, which is attached to the wood with glue, or, in the case of one of the sets, with small brass pins. The pieces measure about ⅞ by ⅝ by ⅜ inch. This set is composed: first, of 3 suits of 21 pieces marked with black and red dots, each comprising the Chinese series without the duplicates; second, of 2 suits of 21 pieces, similarly marked with black and red dots with the addition of ornamental devices of flowers in red and green; third, of 1 suit of 21 pieces, each with double sets of dots, 1 set being placed at each end of the pieces, and between certain devices in red and green, comprising the emblems of the Eight Genii, the characters for "sun" and "moon," a tiger, and various flowers.

A similar set was exhibited by W. H. Wilkinson, esq., Her British Majesty's consul-general, Seoul, Korea, in his collection in the section of games at the Columbian Exposition, Chicago, 1893. They were from Shanghai, and designated as Hua ho (*fá ho*) "flower harmony."‡

Another set (B) in the museum of the Long Island Historical Society comprises 141 marked pieces and 2 blanks. They are made of bamboo with a bone or ivory face, which is skillfully mortised to the wood, and measure ⅞ by ⅝ by ⅜ inch. This set is composed:

First, of 4 suits of 9 pieces each, marked in red, green, and blue, with from 1 to 9 circles.

Second, of 4 suits of 9 pieces each, marked in red and green, with from 1 to 9 narrow rectangles.

Third, of 4 suits of 9 pieces each, marked with the characters *yat mán,* "one ten thousand," to *kau mán,* or "nine ten thousand." The characters for "one" to "nine" are in blue, and that for *mán,* "ten thousand," is in red.

Fourth, of 4 pieces marked *pak,* "north," in blue; of 4 pieces marked *nám,* "south," in blue; of 4 pieces marked *tung,* "east," in blue; of 4

---

* Chinese Reader's Manual, part 2, No. 301.

† The gift of the Hon. George Glover, formerly U. S. consul at Fuhchau. There is a similar collection given by him in the American Museum of Natural History, Central Park, New York.

‡ Cf. Descriptive Catalogue World's Columbian Exposition, Department M, revised edition, p. 87.

pieces marked *sai*, "west," in blue; of 4 pieces marked *chung*, "middle," in blue; 1 piece marked *pak wong*, "northern ruler," in red and blue; 1 piece marked *nám wong*, "southern ruler," in red and blue; 1 piece marked *tung wong*, "eastern ruler," in red and blue; 1 piece marked *sai wong*, "western ruler," in red and blue; 1 piece marked *chung wong*, "middle ruler," in red and blue; 1 piece marked *t'in wong*, "heavenly ruler," in red and blue; 1 piece marked *tí wong*, "earthly ruler," in red and blue; 1 piece marked *yan wong*, "human ruler," in red and blue; 1 piece marked *wo wong*, "harmony ruler," in red and blue; 1 piece marked *ch'un*, "spring," in red; 1 piece marked *há*, "summer," in red; 1 piece marked *ts'au*, "autumn," in red; 1 piece marked *tung*, "winter."

Fifth, of 8 blank pieces.

A set nearly identical with this was also exhibited by Mr. Wilkinson. It lacked the pieces designated as "rulers of the five directions," the *t'in*, *tí*, *yan*, and *wo wong*, and the 4 pieces with the names of the seasons. It had, however, 4 pieces bearing the character *fát*. This set was from Ningpo, and was designated by Mr. Wilkinson as chung fa (*chung fát*). "The coloring," he states, "whether in red, green, or blue, is purely ornamental, and has nothing to do with the play of the game.*

Another set (C), from Fuhchau, in the museum of the Long Island Historical Society, is made entirely of bamboo. This set is composed of 32 pieces, measuring ⅞ by ⁵⁄₁₅ by ³⁄₁₅ inch. They are inscribed on one face with the usual dots and the characters that represent the names of the pieces of the Chinese game of chess, *tséung k'í*.

These marks are arranged as follows:

    6-6 6-6, *kü*, "chariot," in red.
    1-1 1-1, *tséung*, "elephant," in green.
    4-4 4-4, *kü*, "chariot," in red.
    1-3 1-3, *séung*, "elephant," in red.
    5-5 5-5, *tsut*, "soldier," in red.
    3-3 3-3, *ping*, "soldier," in green.
    2-2 2-2, *sz'*, "secretary," in green.
    5-6 5-6, *má*, "horse," in green.
    4-6 4-6, *má*, "horse," in red.
    1-6 1-6, *tsut*, "soldier," in red.
    1-5 1-5, *tsut*, "soldier," in red.
    6-3 4-5, *sz'*, "secretary," in red.
    6-2 5-3, *p'áu*, "cannon," in red.
    4-3 5-2, *p'áu*, "cannon," in green.
    1-4, *ping*, "soldier," in red.
    2-3, *tsut*, "soldier," in red.
    2-4, *tséung*, "general," in green.
    1-2, *shui*, "general," in red.

Mr. Himly† describes a set of Chinese bamboo dominoes, 32 in the set, with the characters of the chessmen, which is identical with the

---

*Descriptive Catalogue, p. 87.
†Zeitschrift des deutscher Morgenländischer Gesellschaft, Band 43, p. 453.

preceding, except for slight variations in the association of the names of the chessmen on the dotted pieces. He offers it in explanation of the number, 32, of the domino game, and says that it could only have been made to save space while traveling. As in the preceding, the 32 dominoes do correspond, piece for piece, with the 32 men in the Chinese game of chess. It is clear that the devices on some, at least, of the other decorated dominoes were copied from playing cards, those on the set A being identical in number as well as in devices with a set of the dotted cards from Fuhchau in the same collection, while the set B has the names of the familiar suit marks, *ping*, *sok*, and *man*, of the cards; hence it is possible that the "chess dominoes" were imitated from the corresponding "chess cards," and that the true explanation of the number of the domino pieces must be found elsewhere.

Mr. W. H. Wilkinson also exhibited at the Columbian Exposition a set of dominoes from Wenchow, called hua tang chiu, " flowery tang chiu." They consist of 5 suits of 21 pieces each and 17 extra pieces (total, 122) and 4 blanks. The extra pieces are (1) 6–6 6–3, (2) 1–1 1–3, (3) 4–4 1–3, (4) 2–4 4–4, (5) 3–3 5–6, (6) 1–2 2–2, (7) 1–2 2–4, (8) 4–5 5–5, (9), (10), (11) 3 pieces marked with the sequence 1–6—that is, 1–4 2–6 3–5; 1–6 2–5 3–4; 1–5 2–3 4–6, and 6 pieces bearing the characters (a) wen, "civilian;" (b) wu, "military;" (c) tsung, "universal;" (d) t'ai, "highness;" (e) ho, "lily;" (f) p'ei, "heap up." "The blanks are used only to replace cards lost." The material was wood, stained black, with incised spots, painted white and red. "The coloring of the cards is immaterial." They measured 1 by $\frac{11}{16}$ by $\frac{3}{16}$ inch, and the inner face was slightly concave, like the dominoes from Fuhchau, mentioned on page 518.*

CH'IÚ P'ÁI.

Another form of Chinese dominoes remains to be described which are current at Tientsin. There are the *ch'iú p'ái*, "leaping dominoes," † which consist of 32 slips of bamboo about 14 inches in length, with the domino spots marked at one end, contained in a cylindrical bamboo box. This game is carried on by cake, candy, and fruit sellers. The player draws 3 of the bamboo slips, and if the 3 marks form what is described under the following account of Korean dominoes, pages 523, 524, as *yat p'ái*, "perfect tablets," the player wins; if not he loses.

KOREAN DOMINOES.

A set of Korean dominoes from Seoul (pl. 9) in the National Museum is made of ivory and numbers 32 pieces. They measure $\frac{3}{4}$ by $\frac{7}{16}$ by $\frac{3}{16}$ inches, and are marked with incised spots arranged according to the Chinese system. The "one" and "four" spots are painted red and all the others black, and the "one" spots are much larger than the others and very deeply incised.

---

* Cf. Descriptive Catalogue, p. 88.
† There is a set from Fuhchau in the museum of the Long Island Historical Society.

The Koreans call dominoes *kŏl-hpai* (Chinese *kwat p'ái*), "bone tablets." A more correct name is said to be *ho-hpai*, (Chinese *Ū p'ái*), "barbarian tablets." This latter name is also applied to a special game. The 32 dominoes are paired as shown in pl. 6, those of which there are two being mated with each other, and those of which there are but one with reference to the sum of the spots, but not in the manner of the Chinese series (Pl. 5).

The pieces receive the same names as those of the dice throws of the Korean game *Ssang-ryouk*, "backgammon," viz:

1-1, *syo-syo* (Chinese *sii ní*), "smallest."
1-2, *tjou-hko* (Chinese *shŭ pí*), "rat nose."
1-3, *syo sam* (Chinese *sá sám*), "small and three."
1-4, *pdik sd* (Chinese *pák sz'*), "white and four."
1-5, *pdik i* (Chinese *pák 'ng*), "white and five."
1-6, *pdik ryouk* (Chinese *pák luk*), "white and six."
2-2, *tjoun-a* (Chinese *tsun á*), "superior two."
2-3, *a sam* (Chinese *á sam*), "two and three."
2-4, *a sd* (Chinese *á sz'*), "two and four."
2-5, *koan-a* (Chinese *kun á*), "sovereign two."
2-6, *a ryouk* (Chinese *á luk*), "two and six."
3-3, *tjyang-sam* (Chinese *ch'éung sám*), "long three."
3-4, *sam sd* (Chinese *sám sz'*), "three four."
3-5, *sam o* (Chinese *sám 'ng*), "three and five."
3-6, *sam ryouk* (Chinese *sám luk*), "three and six."
4-4, *tjoun-hong* (Chinese *tsun hung*), "superior red."
4-5, *sd o* (Chinese *sz' 'ng*), "four and five."
4-6, *sd ryouk* (Chinese *sz' luk*), "four and six."
5-5, *tjoun o* (Chinese *tsun 'ng*), "superior five."
5-6, *o ryouk* (Chinese *'ng luk*), "five and six."
6-6, *tjoun-ryouk* (Chinese *tsun luk*), "superior six."

Dominoes are regarded as a vulgar game in Korea. They are used in gambling houses and are not much played as a social game by the higher classes.

HO-HPAI.

The commonest Korean game of dominoes is called *Ho-hpai*, i. e., "Barbarian tablets." It is played by 3 or 4 persons. When 4 persons play an entire set of dominoes are used. When 3 play the following pieces are withdrawn: 6-6, 5-5, 4-4, and 3-3. The dominoes are turned face down and shuffled. On commencing to play, the players all draw 1 piece to decide who shall play first. The one who gets the piece with the highest number of spots becomes the *Tjyang-ouen* (Chinese, *Chong ün*).[*] The pieces are again shuffled and the *Tjyang-ouen* draws 7 pieces and each of the other players 6. The *Tjyang-ouen* then whirls his 7 pieces about between his fingers in the right hand until 1 piece slips out. This piece he turns face up. Should the piece turned up be either 5-4, 1-2, 1-4 or 2-3 he keeps the pieces he has drawn. If it should be either 6-6, 5-5, 4-4, 3-3, 2-2, 1-1, 6-5, 6-4, 6-1, 5-1, or 3-1, that is to

---

[*] This title is that of the first of the literary graduates in Korea. The same name is applied to the first of the Hanlin doctors in China.

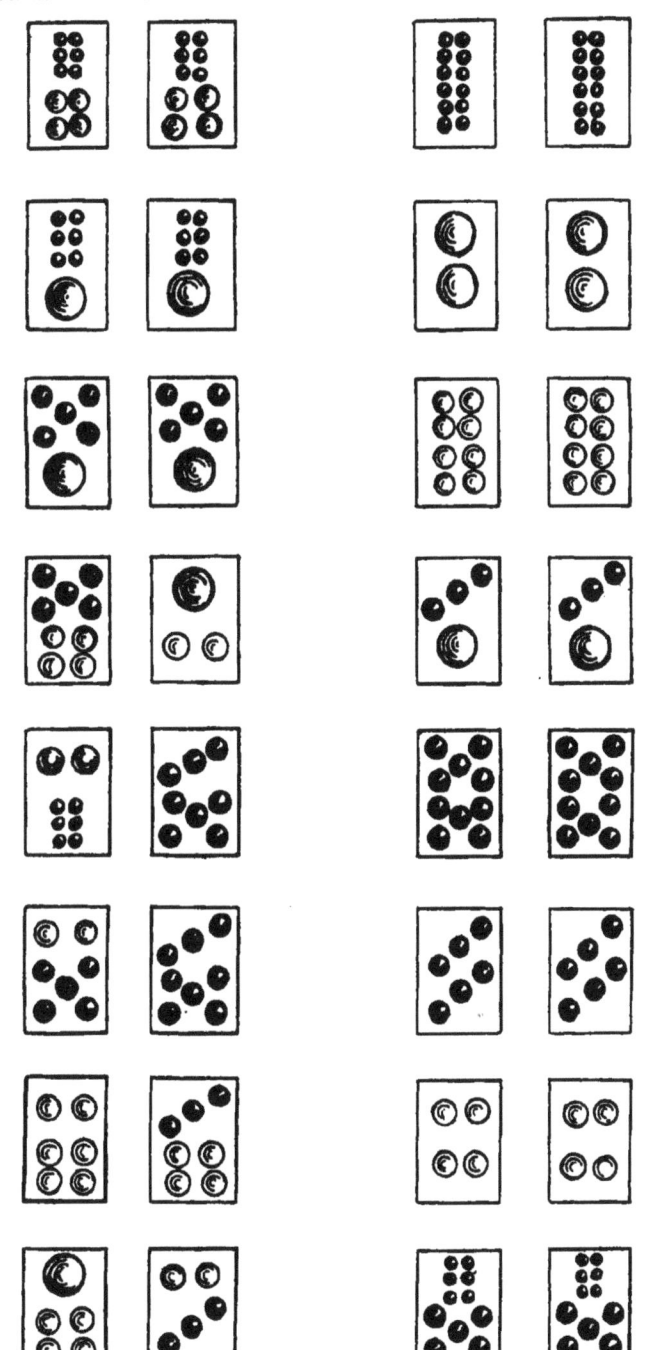

KOREAN DOMINOES.
Cat. No. 77094, U. S. N. M.

say one of the pieces of which there are duplicates, he hands his 6 pieces that are yet undisclosed to the player on his right who in turn gives his pieces to the player next to him, and so on until the *Tjyang-ouen* receives those of the fourth player. If on the other hand, he turns up either 6-3, 6-2, 5-3, 5-2, 4-3, or 4-2, he hands his 6 pieces to the player on the left who in turn gives his pieces to his immediate neighbor until the *Tjyang-ouen* receives those from the player on the right. The seventh piece that was turned up is now turned down and mixed with the remaining pieces, which are placed side by side in a line, and covered with a slip of paper, or a strip of bamboo made for the purpose. If the *Tjyang-ouen* keeps his pieces, he becomes the first player, but if he exchanges them, the one on the right or left to whom he gave his pieces becomes the first player. In this game certain combinations of 3 pieces are called *han-hpai* (Chinese *yat p' ái*), "perfect tablets," and the object of the game is to get 2 such combinations. The game is then spoken of as *hto-tjye-ta*, "broken". *Ho-hpai* is played for money and a certain stake agreed upon, the player winning once, twice, thrice, four or five times this amount for each player, according to the combination which composes his winning hand. These combinations and the numbers they count are as follows:

(1) A sequence, as 1-3, 2-4, 5-6, called *ssang-syo-han-hpai* (Chinese, *shéung tsü yat p'ái*), counts 3 in combination with another *ssang-syo*, and 1, in combination with any other *han-hpai*. A *ssang-syo* composed of 6 pieces, which pair according to the Korean system, is called *tái-sá-ttai* (Chinese, *túi sz' tai*), literally, "corresponding four times," and counts 4, the name referring to the count.

(2) The sequence 1-1, 1-2, 1-3, 1-4, 1-5, 1-6, and the corresponding sequences in which 6, 5, 4, 3 and 2 replace the ones in this example, are called *pou-tong* (Chinese, *pat t'ung*), "unlike," and count as follows:

            1-1, 1-2, 1-3, 1-4, 1-5, 1-6 counts 3.
            2-1, 2-2, 2-3, 2-4, 2-5, 2-6 counts 5.
            3-1, 3-2, 3-3, 3-4, 3-5, 3-6 counts 3.
            4-1, 4-2, 4-3, 4-4, 4-5, 4-6 counts 3.
            5-1, 5-2, 5-3, 5-4, 5-5, 5-6 counts 4.
            6-1, 6-2, 6-3, 6-4, 6-5, 6-6 counts 3.

(3) The sequence 1-2, 3-6, 4-5, 1-4, 2-6, 3-5, called *hol-ssang-syo* (Chinese, *tuk shéung tsü*), "solitary double sequence," counts 5.

(4) Two doublets, and 1 piece upon which the sum of the spots, or 1 of the 2 sets of spots is equal to the single number of the doublets, as 1-4, 5-5, 5-5, or 4-2, 4-4, 4-4, called *sok* (Chinese, *noi*), "inclosed," counts 1, both when paired with another *sok* or any other *han-hpai*. A *han-hpai* composed of sixes is called *ryouk-sok;* of fives, *o-sok;* of fours, *hong-sok;* of threes, *sam-sok;* of twos, *a-sok*, and of ones, *páik-sok*.

(5) Three pieces upon which the spots are equally divided between 2 numbers, as 4-4, 2-4, 2-2, called *tai-sam-tong* (Chinese, *túi sám t'ung*), "three alike, opposite," count 1.

(6) The combination 6–6, 5–5, 4–4, called *ro-in* (Chinese, *lò yan*), "old man," counts 3 when combined with itself and 1 with any other *han-hpai*. The combination 3–3, 2–2, 1–1, called *a-ki* (Chinese, *á chí*), "child," counts 3 when combined with itself and 1 with any other *han-hpai*.

(7) The combination 6–6, 3–3, 2–2, called *ssang-pyen* (Chinese, *shéung pín*), "doublets," counts 3 when combined with itself and 1 with any other *han-hpai*. The combinations 2–3, 3–1, 1–2, and 4–5, 5–6, 4–6, called *Yo-Soun*, count 3 when combined with each other and 1 in combination with any other *han-hpai*.

As the *sok* are combinations which may be formed very easily, it is sometimes agreed to play without them. If the first player has not drawn a winning hand he puts down a piece from his hand at the end that is nearest to him of the concealed row and takes up the piece at the other end, at the same time sliding the row of pieces along, so that the piece he puts down is concealed, and the piece he takes up is exposed. If he then does not make a winning combination, the next player, if he has not already a winning combination, puts down a piece and takes up another as before, and this is continued until some one obtains a winning combination, and so wins the game. He then becomes the *Tjyang-ouen* in the next game.

TJAK-MA-TCHI-KI.

Tjak-ma-tchi-ki, "pair making," is played by 2, 3, or 4 persons. The pieces are reversed and shuffled and covered with paper. The first player draws 6 and the other players each draw 5 dominoes. The first player endeavors to play out a pair from those he has drawn, but if he is unsuccessful he lays out 1 piece face up on the table. The second player takes up the piece discarded if he can combine it with a domino in his hand to form a pair. If not, he draws a piece from those left under the paper, and discards a domino, which he lays out face up. This process is continued around until 1 player gets 3 pairs in his hand, and becomes the winner. When 2 or 3 play, the 6–6 can not be played to complete the third pair, but when 4 play it may thus be played and the winner must be paid alone by the player who discarded the corresponding piece.

If the pair is completed by a piece drawn from the unused pile, all the other players pay the winner, but if it is completed by a piece which has been discarded, the player who discarded that piece alone pays the winner. It is sometimes agreed that the third pair by which a player wins must be completed with a piece drawn from the unused pile.

KKO-RI-POUT-TCHI-KI.

Kko-ri-pout-tchi-ki, "tail joining," is played by 2, 3, or 4 persons; 3 or 4 usually play. The set of dominoes are reversed and shuffled and each player draws 8 dominoes. When 3 play, the pieces 6–6, 5–5, 4–4, and

3-3 are first withdrawn. The game is begun by someone asking who has the *koan a*? The holder of this piece, the 5-2, lays down any piece he may select from his hand, face up, at the same time crying out a number on one side of it, which number must be paired. The next player must mate the side designated with one of his pieces, but if unable to do so, must lay a piece from his hand, face down on the table. The game is continued around until all have been paired or all have laid down their pieces. Then each counts the spots on the pieces they have been compelled to lay down, which naturally have been selected from those with the fewest spots in their hands, and the one who has the highest number of spots pays the one who has the lowest number of spots. When 4 play, all players who count more than 30 must pay.

KŎL-YE-SI.*

Kŏl-ye-si is played by two or more persons, not exceeding ten. The set of dominoes is placed face down and shuffled, and part, if not all of the set, are placed end to end in an irregular line. One of the players acts as banker, *Moul-tjyou* (Chinese, *Mat chü* "things' ruler"). The other players each draw 1 piece in turn from the line. They examine this piece and each put whatever stake they choose on the piece drawn. The *Moul-tjyou* puts down the same amount, whatever it may be, beside each player's stake and takes the next 2 pieces. If his pieces are identical, a perfect pair, he at once wins all that has been staked. Otherwise the other players draw in turn either 1 or 2 pieces from the line. This done, they and the *Moul-tjyou* turn their pieces face up. They all count the spots on their dominoes. The remainders, after deducting the tens, count, and if the *Moul-tjyou* has an excess over that of any player, he takes the stakes, but if a player has an excess over that of the *Moul-tjyou* when the tens are deducted from the sum of the spots, that player wins the amount of the stake he has staked.

This is a common game in gambling houses. It is customary to keep a water jar there, in which the players voluntarily put a portion of their stakes before the result is disclosed, or, if unmindful, at the suggestion of some one interested in the house.

RYONG-HPAI.

Dominoes are used in Korea as in China in playing solitaire, which, as in China, is a favorite kind of sortilage, not regarded seriously, but often played at the beginning of the day, the player wishing for a happy omen. The solitaire game described under the name of *hoi t'áp*, page 516, is known under the name of *Ryong-hpai* (Chinese, *lung p'ái*), "Dragon tablets," while another arrangement is shown in fig. 20.

Kŏl-ye-si means *kŏl* (*hpai*) or "domino" *ye-si*, the latter being the name of a game played with cards.

526   REPORT OF NATIONAL MUSEUM, 1893.

KE-POUK-HPAI.

In this system, called *ke-pouk-hpai* (Chinese, *kwai p'ái*), "Tortoise tablets," the 32 dominoes are laid face down to form a representation of a tortoise (fig. 21), with 2 pieces at head and tail and 2 for legs at each of the 4 corners. The pieces at these extremities are turned face up, followed by those marked A, B, C, D, and mated according to the Korean system, (pl. 9). The player loses when he fails to mate all the pieces.

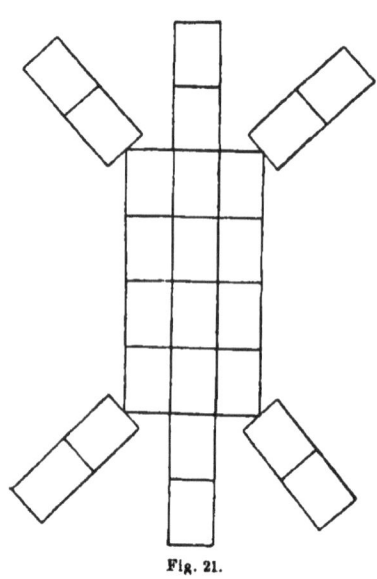

SIN-SYO-TYEN.

Sin-syo-tyen (Chinese, *shan shò chím*), "personally counting divination," is a kind of fortune telling practiced with dominoes. The inquirer shuffles a set of dominoes face down and arranges them side by side in a line. He then turns them face up, preserving the arrangement, and selects as many of the combinations referred to on pages 523, 524, as can be formed by

Fig. 21.
ARRANGEMENT OF DOMINOES IN KE-POUK-HPAI, "TORTOISE TABLETS." KOREA.

contiguous pieces. The sum of the numbers there given, in connection with the combinations thus formed is noted, and the operation twice repeated. The three results are added together, and if their sum amounts to 32, the number of the domino pieces, the augury is very good; more or less being estimated proportionally good or indifferent.

O-KOAN.

Another popular method of divination with dominoes is called *o-koan* (Chinese, *'ng kwán*), "5 gateways."

An entire set of 8 dominoes is reversed and shuffled and 20 pieces are then arranged face down in 5 rows of 4 pieces each (fig. 22). The player then turns these pieces face up and commencing at the bottom row endeavors to form combinations of 3 pieces each, *han-hpai* such as have been described under *ho-hpai* In addition to the *han-hpai* already enumerated, pages

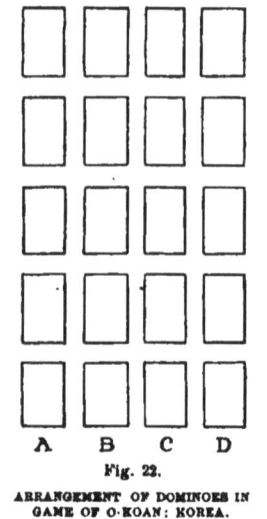

A   B   C   D
Fig. 22.
ARRANGEMENT OF DOMINOES IN GAME OF O-KOAN: KOREA.

523, 524, the following additional ones are permitted in *o-koan:* Three pieces upon which 3 of the spots are alike and the sum of the other 3 spots is equal to 5, called *sam-tong-tan-o-tyem* (Chinese *sám t'ung tán 'ng tím*), "three alike and only five spots," and 3 pieces upon which 3 of the spots are alike and the sum of the other 3 spots is equal to or more than 14, called *sam-tong-sip-sá-tyem* (Chinese *sám t'ung shap sz' tím*), "three alike and fourteen spots."

In forming these combinations, 3 contiguous pieces in a row may be taken, or 1 or 2 pieces at one end of a row may be used in combination with 2 pieces or 1 piece at the other end, the pieces thus taken being always placed on the inner side. Thus the piece A may be mated with C D to form a combination A C D, or B A may be mated with D to form a combination A B D. The combinations thus formed are removed and placed in a line face up above the 5 rows, the one found nearest the bottom being placed to the left and successive ones to the right of the line thus started. When no more combinations can be discovered, 5 pieces are drawn from the unused pile of 12 pieces which have been left with their faces down, and one of them placed face down to the right of each of the 5 rows. These 5 pieces are then turned face up, and an attempt made to form combinations of threes with their aid. The results are successively placed to the right of the line at the top and this process is continued until the 12 extra pieces are exhausted. When this happens, 5 pieces are withdrawn from the left of the top line and added in succession to right of the 5 rows. If, by chance, but 4 or a less number of rows remain, only a corresponding number of pieces are drawn. This process is continued over and over until all the pieces are combined in sets of threes in a long row at the top, or the top row is exhausted and a block ensues, determining success or failure. The name of the game is said to have been taken from a well-known episode in the life of *Koan Ou*[*] (Chinese, *Kwán Ü*), the

---

[*] Kwan Yü (*Kwán Ü*) D. A. D. 219. Designated Kwan Chwáng Miú and deified as Kwan Ti or Wu Ti, the God of War. A native of Kiai Chow, in Shan-si, who rose to celebrity toward the close of the second century through his alliance with Liu Pei and Chang Fei in the struggles which ushered in the period of the Three Kingdoms. He is reputed to have been, in early life, a seller of bean-curd, but to have subsequently applied himself to study until, in A. D. 184, he casually encountered Liu Pei at a time when the latter was about to take up arms in defense of the house of Han against the rebellion of the Yellow Turbans. He joined Liu Pei and his confederate, Chang Fei, in a solemn oath, which was sworn in a peach-orchard belonging to the latter, that they would fight henceforth side by side and live and die together. The fidelity of Kwan Yü to his adopted leaders remained unshaken during a long series of years in spite of many trials; and similarly his attachment to Chang Fei continued throughout his life. At an early period of his career he was created a t'ing how (baron) by the regent Ts'ao Ts'ao, with the title of Hán shu t'ing hau. * * * His martial powers shone conspicuously in many campaigns which were waged by Liu Pei before his throne as sovereign of Shu became assured, but he fell a victim at last to the superior force and strategy of Sun K'üan, who took him prisoner and caused him to be beheaded. Long celebrated as one of the most renowned among China's heroes, he was at length canonized by the superstitious Hwei T'sung, of the Sung dynasty, early in the Twelfth century, with the title Chung hwui Kung. In 1128 he received the still higher title of Chwáng miú wu ngán wáng, and after many subsequent alterations and additions he was at length raised in 1594 by Ming Wan Li to the rank of Ti, or God, since which date, and especially since the accession of the Manchow dynasty, his worship as the God of War has been firmly established. (Chinese Reader's Manual, No. 297.)

celebrated Chinese general, now universally worshiped in China as the God of War, and one of the heroes of the famous historical romance, the *Sám Kwok chí*, or "Annals of Three States." In escaping from Ts'ao Ts'ao,* it is recorded that he killed six generals at "five frontier passes," *o-koan* (Chinese *'ng kwán*). The vicissitudes of his life at this time are typified in the varying fortunes of the game, which at one moment approaches a successful termination, only for the player to be unexpectedly set back to overcome its obstacles anew. The conquest of the "five *koan*," which *Koan Ou* achieved, finds it analogue in the 5 rows of the dominoes which the player struggles to overcome. Many educated people play this game every morning, and scholars who have nothing to do play it all day long, finding intellectual pastime in its elusive permutations.

BURMESE AND SHAN DOMINOES.

A set of Burmese dominoes in the National Museum are of teak wood and measure 2 by 1 by ⅜ inches (pl. 10). The spots are marked with incised circles. They number 24 pieces, marked as follows: 6-6, 1-1, 4-4, 1-3, 5-5, 3-3, and 2-2 duplicated, and one each of the following pieces: 6-3, 4-5, 6-2, 5-3, 4-3, 5-2, 2-4, 1-4, 2-3, and 1-2, the last having 2 smaller spots adjoining the "1."

They are accompanied by a cubical die about three-fourths inch square, with 2 opposite faces marked with 1 spot, 2 opposite faces marked with 2 spots, and 2 opposite faces marked with 3 spots. This is used to decide who shall play first.

A set of Burmese dominoes, from Rangoon, sent to the writer by the Hon. Sir C. H. T. Crosthwaite, lieutenant-general Northwest Provinces, British India, are identical with the preceding, except that the spots are marked with small brass disks.

A set of Burmese dominoes in the British Museum are made of black horn, and number 32 pieces. They measure 1⅜ inches in length by three-fourths of an inch in width and have incised spots, which are painted red and yellow and arranged according to the Chinese system. The backs are uniformly marked with "1" and "3" spots composed of concentric circles, and the ends each bear 1 spot similarly inscribed. Another set of Burmese dominoes in the same collection are made of black wood, with the spots painted red and white.

Dice are called *anzamiá* (singular *anzá*) in Burmese. The Burmese dice in the museum of the University of Pennsylvania are small ivory cubes, regularly marked and having the fours in red, and are identical with the Chinese.

A set of Shan dominoes in the British Museum, presented by Maj. E. B. Gladen, are identical in every respect with the horn dominoes from Burma in the same museum.

---

*Ts'ao Ts'ao *D.*, A. D. 220. Chinese Reader's Manual, No. 768.

Report of National Museum, 1893.—Culin. PLATE 10.

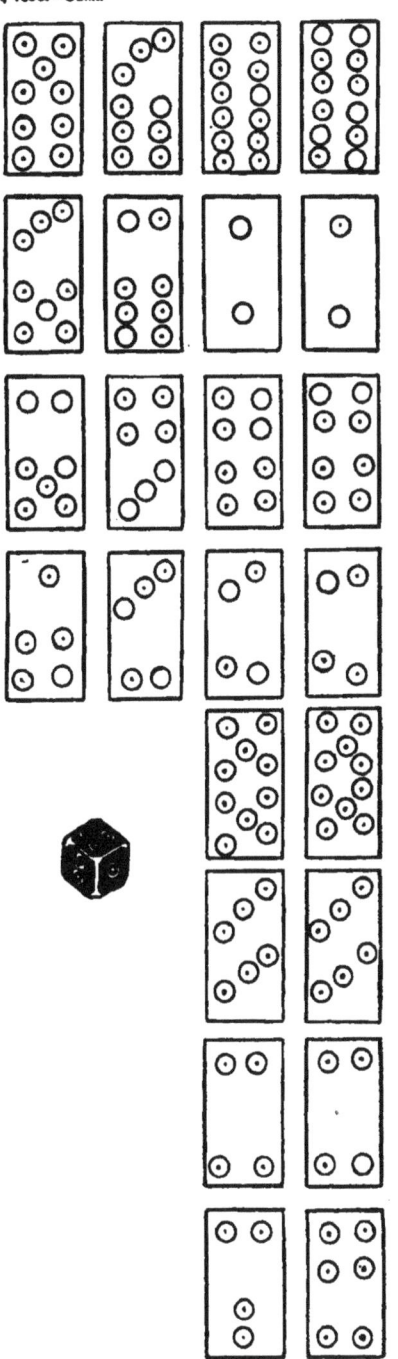

BURMESE DOMINOES.
Cat. No. 166540, U. S. N. M.

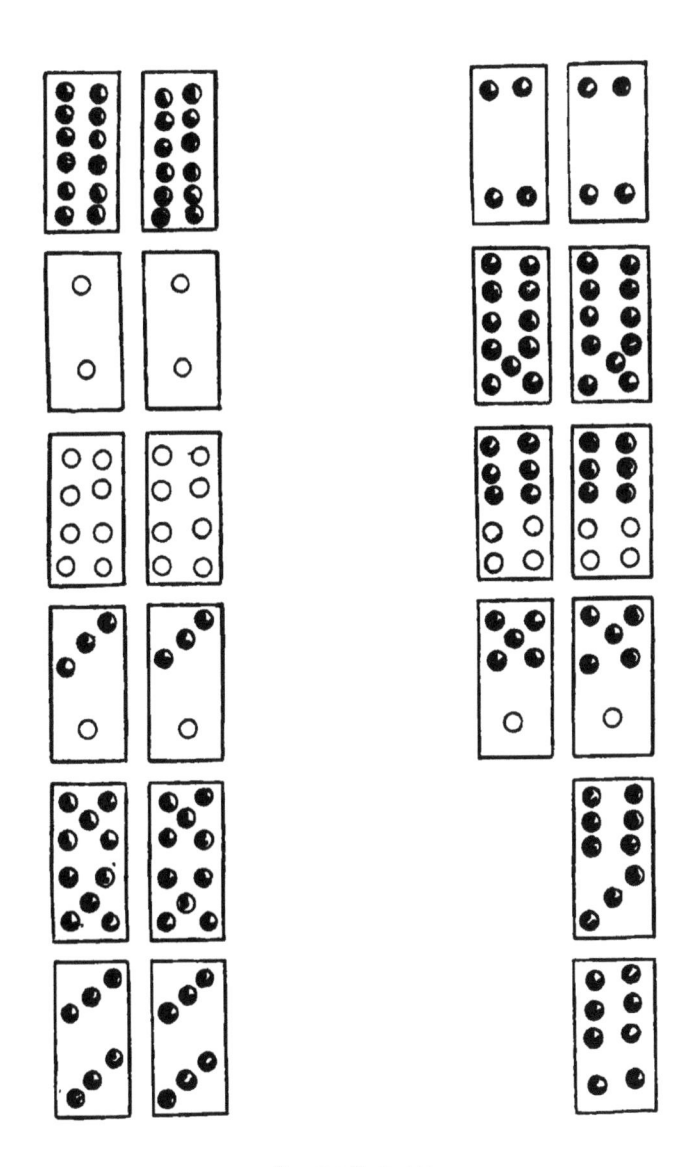

SIAMESE DOMINOES.

SIAMESE DOMINOES.

Dominoes are called in Siamese *tau tem* (Chinese *tá tím*) "arranging or connecting spots." Two sets of dominoes exhibited by the Government of Siam in the Section of Games at the Columbian Exposition consist of 24 thin rectangular tablets of ivory, one with face of 1½ by ⅜, and the other 1¹¹⁄₁₆ by ⅝ inches (pl. 11). The "ones" and "fours" are marked with red and the others with black spots, in the following series: The pieces 6-6, 1-1, 4-4, 1-3, 5-5, 3-3, 2-2, 5-6, 4-6, 1-6, and 1-5 duplicated, and one of each of the pieces 6-3 and 6-2.

ESKIMO DOMINOES.

A set of Innuit dominoes in the U. S. National Museum, Washington, (pl. 12), is described by Mr. Lucien Turner, who conducted the expedition for the Smithsonian Institution in 1884.[*]

"The Innuit," Mr. Turner says, "who come from the western end of Hudson Strait, the so-called Northerners, have a game which they play with sets of pieces of ivory cut into irregular shapes, and marked on one face with spots arranged in different patterns. The number of pieces in a set varies from 60 to 148. The name of a set is *A ma si a lát*, and somewhat resembles our game of dominoes.

"The game is played in the following manner: Two or more persons, according to the number of pieces in the set, sit down and pile the pieces before them. One of the players mixes the pieces together in plain view of the others. When this is done he calls them to take the pieces. Each person endeavors to obtain a half or third of the number, if there be two or three players. The one who mixed up the pieces lays down a piece and calls his opponent to match it with a piece having a similar design. If this can not be done by any of the players the first has to match it, and the game continues until one of the players has exhausted all of the pieces taken by him. The pieces are designated by pairs, having names such as *ka mǐsi tǐk* (sled), *kaiak* (canoe), *kalǐ sak* (navel), *á ma sut* (many), *a tai sǐk* (1), *má kok* (2), *pǐng a sut* (3), *si tǐ mút* (4), and *tá li mat* (5). Each of the names above must be matched with a piece of similar kind, although the other end of the piece may be of a different design. A *kamutik* may be matched with an *amasut*, if the latter has not a line or bar cut across it; if it has a bar it must be matched with an *amasut*.

"This game is known to the people of the Ungava district, but those only who learn it from the Northerners are able to play it. The northern Eskimo stake the last article they possess on the issue of the game. Their wives are disposed of temporarily, and often are totally relinquished to the victor. I have heard of wives so disposed of often sit down and win themselves back to their former owners."

Dr. Franz Boas informs me that the Eskimo name for dominoes means "standing upright side by side."

MISCELLANEOUS GAMES.

Several fanciful games have come to my notice which have been suggested by the European domino game. In the Section of Games in the Department of Anthropology at the Columbian Exposition, Chicago, 1893, a modern French game was exhibited under the name of *Le Magister Dominoes Geographique*, consisting of oblong pieces of cardboard, each bearing on its face a portion of the map of the Valley of the Seine. It was intended to be used for teaching geography. Another game,

---

[*] Eleventh Annual Report of the Bureau of Ethnology, 1889-'90, pp. 257-258.

entitled "Evan's Baseball Dominoes," consisted of wooden domino-shaped blocks marked on one face at the ends with the names of the scoring points in the American game of baseball.

INTRODUCTION OF DOMINOES INTO EUROPE.

From the foregoing accounts it will be seen how widely the peculiar Chinese game of dominoes is distributed, from Korea to Burma and Siam. Dr. Gustav Schlegel states that the European game of dominoes is without doubt borrowed from the Chinese, only that in it the philosophic-astronomic elements have been done away with and only the arithmetical retained. I have been unable to discover the connecting links between the two games. The Levant may furnish a clew to the relationship if any such now exists, but I am without information on the subject.

The game seems to date from a recent period in Europe. According to Brockhaus' Conversations-Lexicon, Art "Domino," it was introduced into Germany through France from Italy about the middle of the last century. In England it appears from a writer in Notes and Queries [*] to have been introduced by French prisoners about the close of the last century.

INVENTION OF THE GAME.

According to a tradition current among the Chinese laborers in the United States, dominoes were invented by *Hung Ming*,[†] a hero of that popular romance, the *Sám Kwok chi*,[‡] for the amusement of his soldiers to keep them awake during the watches of the night in their camp before the enemy. Others attribute them to the ingenuity of *Kéung t'ái Kung*,[§] and give a similar reason for their discovery. A Chinese physician, the most scholarly of my informants among his class, insisted that they were invented by *Fán Lai*,[||] whose picture, from a popular illustrated edition of the *Tung chau lit kwok*,[¶] is reproduced in fig. 23. Little importance need be attached to these stories, which are given as illustrations of the conflicting statements made by the comparatively uneducated Chinese regarding things which are a matter of record.

Dr. Gustav Schlegel,[**] quoting from the Chi sz yin kau (*Chü sz' yám káu*),[††] states that dominoes were invented in 1120 A. D. by a statesman

---

[*] January 23, 1869.

[†] Chu-ko Liang (*Hung Ming*), A. D. 181–234. The great counselor of Liu Pei, who owed to the sagacity and military skill of Chu-ko Liang his success in establishing himself upon the throne. (The Chinese Reader's Manual, No. 88.)

[‡] Wylie, A., Notes on Chinese Literature, Shanghai, 1867, p. 161.

[§] Kiang Tsze-ya (*Kéung t'ái kung*) is reported to have been a counselor of Si Peh, twelfth century B. C. (The Chinese Reader's Manual, No. 257.)

[||] Fan Li (*Fán Lai*), minister of Kow Tsien, Prince of Yüeh, whom he aided to overthrow the rival kingdom of Wu, the final victory of which, after twenty years' warfare, was achieved B. C. 473. (The Chinese Reader's Manual, No. 127.)

[¶] Notes on Chinese Literature, p. 162.

[**] Chinesische Bräuch und Spiele in Europa, Breslau, 1869, p. 18.

[††] Investigations on the traditions of all things.

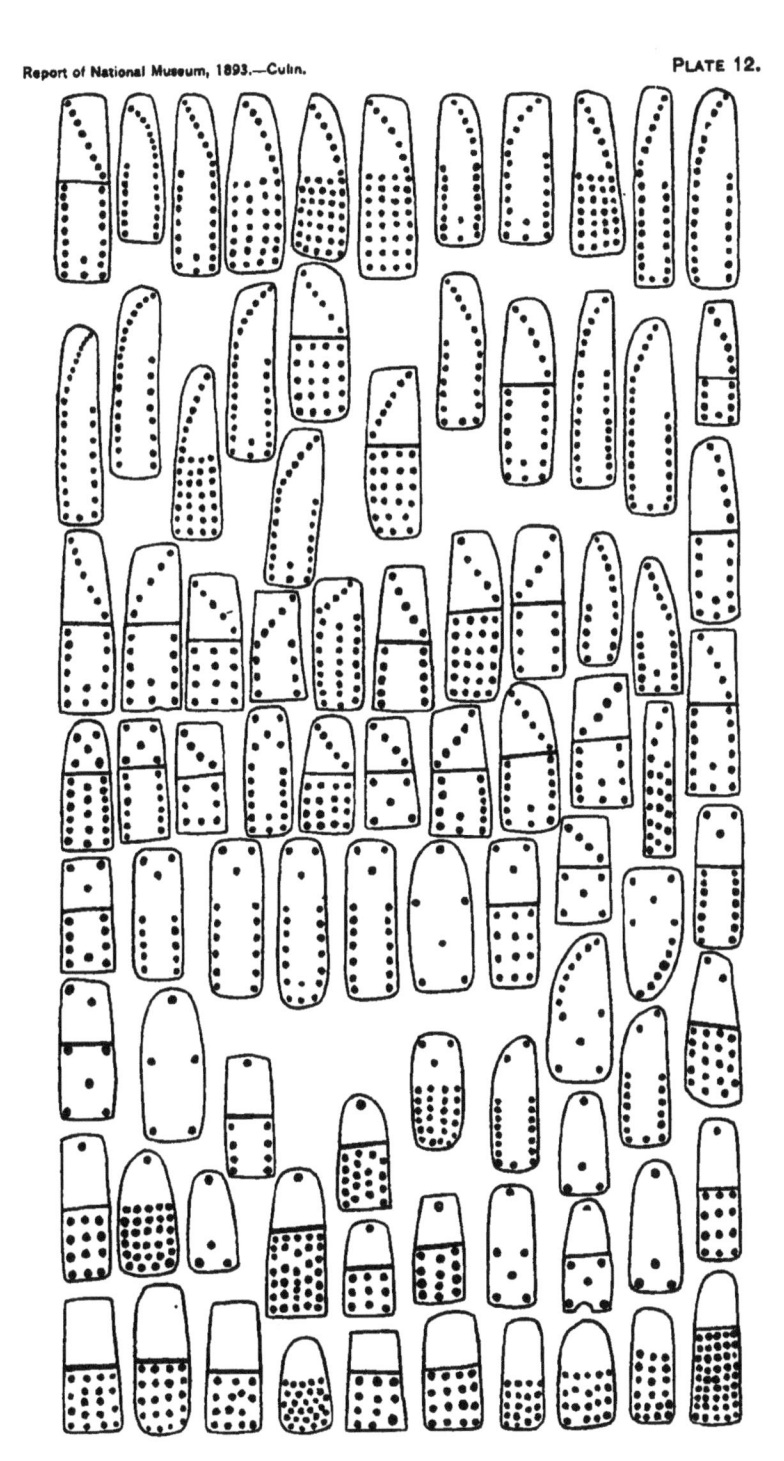

ESKIMO DOMINOES.
Cat. No. 76880, U. S. N. M.

who presented them to the Emperor Hwui-tsung, and that the game with its explanation was locked in the imperial treasury and first came into general use in the reign of Hwui-tsung's son, Kao-tsung (1127-1163 A. D.).

Mr. Karl Himly* cites Kánghí's Dictionary as saying that according to general tradition dominos were invented in the second year of Siuen-ho (1120) and circulated abroad by imperial order at the time of Kao-tsung.

Mr. Chatto † quotes the other great Chinese dictionary of the last century, the Ching tsz' t'ung, on the authority of Mr. Samuel Birch, as saying that the cards now known in China as "Teen-tsze-pae" (tim tsz' p'ái), or "dotted cards," were invented in the reign of Siuen-ho, 1120, and that they began to be common in the reign of Kao-tsung.

Mr. W. H. Wilkinson has recently shown ‡ that in the citation made by Chatto from the Ching tsz' tung, he omits the concluding and most important sentence: "It does not follow that this class of games originated in the period Hsüan-ho," and says that the passage, adduced again and again by European writers to prove that cards (dominoes) were first invented in the reign of Siuen-ho, when carefully examined, distinctly declares that such a conclusion would be unsound.

"It is perfectly clear," Mr. Wilkinson says, "that all that was done or asked for in 1120 was an imperial decision as to which of several forms of T'ien-kiu (Heavens and Nines) was to be considered orthodox. The game and the cards must have been in existence long before. The passage from the Cheng-tză-t'ung runs thus: 'Also ya p'ai, now the instruments of a game. A common legend states that in the second year of the Hsüan-ho, in the Sung dynasty (1120 A. D.), a certain official memorialized the

Fig. 23.
FÁN LAI.

throne, praying that the ya p'ai (ivory cards) might be fixed as a pack of 32, comprising 127 pips (sic, it should be 227, but Chinese printers are careless), in order to accord with the expanse of the stars and constellations. The combination, 'Heaven,' (6—6, 6—6) consisted of two pieces, containing 24 pips, figures of the 24 solar periods; 'earth' (1—1, 1—1) also composed of two pieces, but contained 4 pips, the four points of the compass—east, west, south and north; 'man' (4—4, 4—4) two pieces, containing 16 pips, the virtues of humanity, benevolence, propriety and wisdom, fourfold; 'harmony' (1—3, 1—3) two pieces of eight pips, figuring the breath of 'Harmony' which pervades the eight divisions of the year. The other combinations had each their names. There were four players having 8 cards apiece for their hand, and the cards won or lost according as the number of the pips was less or more, the winner being rewarded with counters. In the time of Kao-tsung

---

* Zeitschrift der deutscher Morgenländischen Gesellschaft, Band 43, p. 451.
† Facts and Speculations on the History of Playing Cards. London, 1848, p. 55.
‡ The American Anthropologist, Jan., 1895, vol. viii., No. 1, p. 66.

(1127-1163) pattern packs were issued by imperial edict. They are now known throughout the empire as ku p'ai, 'bone pai;' but it does not follow that this class of games, po-sai, ko-wu, and the rest originated in the reign Hsüan-ho."

As the foregoing shows that the historical evidence is inconclusive as to the actual invention of dominoes, and as the Chinese accounts of the invention of other games are not particularly trustworthy, and especially as the history of all games seems to be one of gradual evolution, rather than direct invention, the following pages are devoted

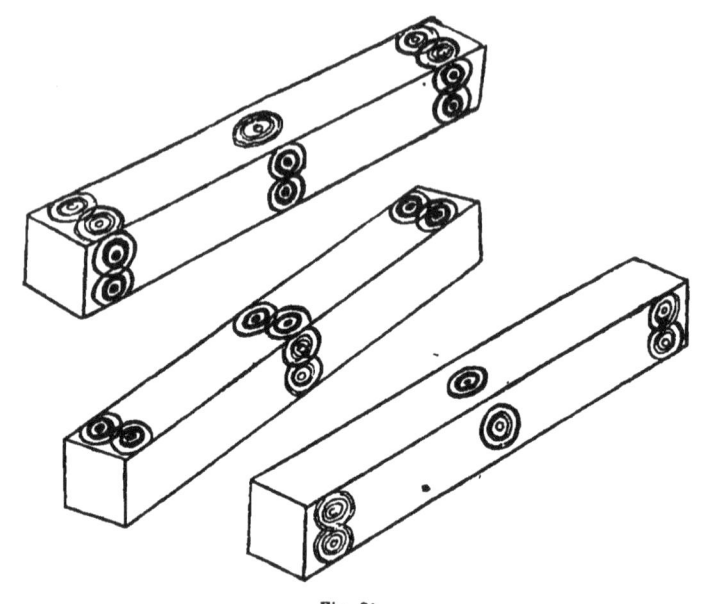

Fig. 24.
PASE (DICE). SET OF THREE FOR CHAUSAR, LUCKNOW, INDIA.
(From specimens in Museum of University of Pennsylvania.)

to an examination into the origin of the game from internal evidences rather than an historical point of view.

DOMINOES A FORM OF DICE.

It is readily apparent that the 21 individual domino pieces represent the possible throws with 2 dice, and that the domino pieces may be regarded as conjoined dice. Of this the Korean dominoes furnish the best material evidence. Consonant with many other Korean objects, they are typical of an earlier age of Chinese culture than that now existing in China.

Their material, color of spots, and the manner in which the "one" spots are incised and made larger than the other spots, complete their resemblance to 2 conjoined dice. If we accept this theory the bone-faced bamboo dominoes may be regarded as directly related to the preceding, the wooden backs being substituted as a matter of economy. Dominoes made entirely of wood would naturally follow, and the long dominoes used in the south of China might be regarded as a later type. Even they bear a suggestion of their origin in the spots with which their ends and tops are decorated.

The names of the dominoes are the same as those of the corresponding throws with the 2 dice, and the pieces are divided, like the dice-throws, into the series of *man* and *mò*, in which they rank in the same order as the dice. The correspondence extends to the game as well, the most characteristic domino game, *tá t'ín kau*, closely resembling the most characteristic dice game, *chák t'ín kau*. Indeed, if dominoes were invented for the purpose of a game, they doubtless had their origin in the game with 2 dice. This game with 2 dice, *shéung luk*, which, according to one Chinese authority, is said to have come from India, finds a parallel in an Indian dice game.

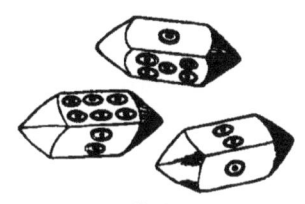

Fig. 25.
PASE (DICE), SET OF THREE FOR CHAUSAR, LUCKNOW, INDIA.
(From specimens in Museum of University of Pennsylvania.)

Several kinds of dice are employed in games in India. One (fig. 24) called *pase* (plural of *pasa*) are used in the game called *chausar*, and consist of rectangular bone or ivory prisms, marked on 4 sides with 1, 2, 5, and 6 spots. These dice are sometimes made shorter and pointed at the ends (fig. 25). Their origin I assign to the staves referred to on page 507. Another kind of Indian dice, called by the Arabic name of *k'ab*, or *kabat*, from *k'ab*, "ankle," "ankle bone," are used in the game of *k'abatain*, 2 dice being thrown. Either natural astragali, consisting of the knuckle bones of a goat, or dice marked on 4 sides with "three," "four," "one," and "six" spots, or cubical dice regularly marked on the 6 sides (fig. 27) are employed. The "four" spots on these

Fig. 26.
SET OF LONG DICE: CELEBES.

dice are usually marked in red, and often both the "three" and "four" are marked in this color.[*] Thus cubical dice appear to be

---

[*] This account of *k'ab* was communicated to the writer by the Hon. Syad Mohammed Hadi, of Sultanpur, India. Two sets of ivory dice, received by the writer from Lucknow, are cubical, and marked on their 6 sides with from 1 to 6 spots, in the same manner as our common dice. The "fours" alone are in red.

directly connected with the knuckle bones. The Arabic name for the knuckle bone and the die is the same, k'ab, and, like the knuckle bones, which are commonly thrown in pairs, natural pairs from the right and left leg being used, cubical dice are also thrown in pairs. Carrying out the resemblance, cubical dice in India are sold in pairs, and by varying the arrangement of the "threes" and "fours"* are actually made in pairs, rights and lefts, like the knuckle bones. If this is the true history of the descent of the cubical dotted die, its evolution must have occurred at a very early time, as the regularly marked stone die from the Greek colony of Naucratis, Egypt (fig. 28), assigned by the discoverer, Mr. Flinders Petrie, to 600° B. C., bears witness.

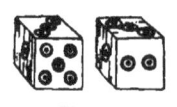

Fig. 27.
KABATAIN—PAIR OF IVORY DICE: LUCKNOW, INDIA.
(From specimens in Museum of University of Pennsylvania.)

Now, the 4 sides of the knuckle bone (*talus*) (fig. 30), which were designated among the Romans as *supinum, pronum, planum*, and *tortuosum*, and correspond with the numbers "three," "four," "one," and "six," receive in the Mohammedan East the names of ranks and conditions of men. The Persians, according to Dr. Hyde,† name them, respectively, "*duzd*," "slave," "*dihban*," "peasant," "*vezir*," "viceroy," and *shah*, or *padi-shah*, "king." Similar names are given by the same author as applied to them by the Arabs, Turks, and Armenians. From this it appears that the names and rank given to the significant throws, "three," "four," "one," and "six," with knuckle bones and dice in Western Asia find their counterparts in the names and rank of the same throws in China, the names of the classes of human society found among the Arabs being replaced in China with the terms for the cosmic powers: "Heaven" ("six"), "Earth" ("one"), and "Man" ("four"), and the "Harmony" ("three-one"), that unites them. It will also be observed that the use of 2 dice, which appears to follow that of the natural pair of knuckle bones, and is displayed in the Indian *k'abatain*, and the ancient and widely diffused game of backgammon, is paralleled by the use of 2 dice in China, where *shéung luk* (Japanese, *sugoroku*)

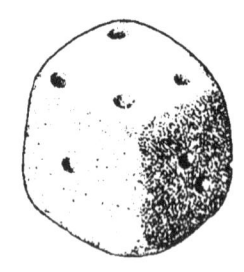

Fig. 28.
STONE DIE: NAUCRATIS, EGYPT.
From specimen in Museum of University of Pennsylvania.

---

* If a Chinese die be turned ace up and revolved toward the person holding it so that the "two," "five," and "six" are disclosed in succession, it will be found that the "three" is usually to the left and the "four" to the right, while the opposite is more usually the case on European dice. In the Indian dice here referred to, this arrangement is alternated, one having the "three" on the right and the other on the left.

† De Ludis Orientalibus, p. 147.

is a common name for dice play. It has been observed that the "threes" and "fours" are marked in red on Indian dice, while in China the "ones" and "fours" are so marked. The *Wak kan san*

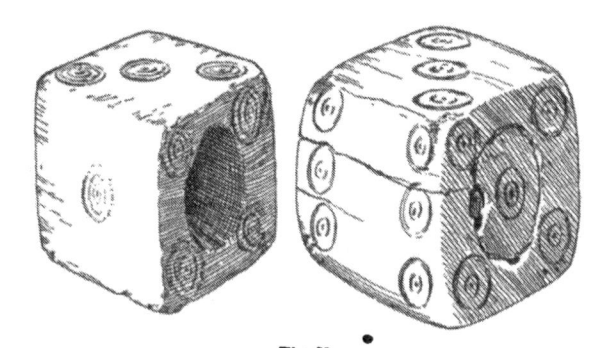

Fig. 29.
ANCIENT ROMAN DICE OF IVORY.
(From specimens in Museum of University of Pennsylvania.)

san relates that in the game of *Sugoroku* the throws receive the following names:

Chō ichi, "double one." Shu shí, "vermilion four."
Chō ni, "double two."   Chō go, "double five."
Shu san, "vermilion three." Chō roku, "double six."

From this it would appear that the dice anciently used in Japan and China had the "three" and "four" marked in red* like the Indian

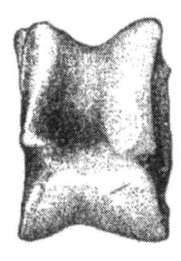

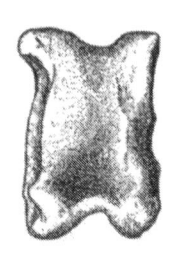

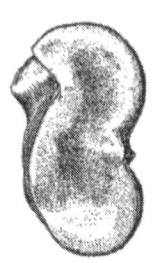

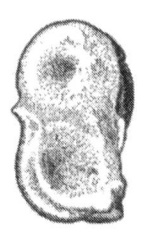

Fig. 30.
THE FOUR SIDES OF A KNUCKLE BONE.
After Hyde.

k'abat, instead of the "one" and "four," as is the present custom—an additional argument in favor of the Indian origin of the Chinese dice. Two questions remain to be answered:

---

*A pair of miniature Japanese ivory dice, presented to the writer by Prof. Henry H. Giglioli, of Florence, Italy, have the "threes" and "fours" marked in red.

Where and for what purpose were the dice-throws united in the domino form, and why was the number of the domino pieces increased from 21 to 32? Dominoes are unknown in India as a native game, but as it seemed possible that they might have had their origin there for use in fortune telling, the writer made a careful examination of the principal East Indian systems of fortune telling with dice, but the results did not throw any light upon the origin of dominoes.* The Thibetan astrologers, according to Schlagintweit,† use dice which are either cubes like European ones, or rectangular parallelopipedons, sometimes comparatively very long; the latter, in consequence of their form, having two sides blank. This description agrees with the preceding Indian dice used in fortune telling, which I regard as derived from the game with staves, but the faces of a die (fig. 32), which Schlagintweit figures as used by the Thibetans for astrological purposes, suggests a domino in the duplication of its spots.‡

Fig. 31.
ANCIENT GLASS ASTRAGALI: SYRIA.
(From specimens in Museum of University of Pennsylvania.)

The astrological associations of the domino game have not thrown

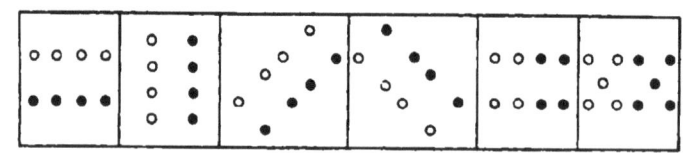

Fig. 32.
FACES OF TIBETAN DIE USED FOR ASTROLOGICAL PURPOSES.
From Schlagintweit.

light as yet upon the question of its origin. They have been referred to in connection with the method of telling fortunes, and it has been observed that the disks accompanying the bamboo dominoes from Fuhchau bear the names of the cyclical animals. It will also be noticed that the terms *ün* and *ngáng*, "weak" and "strong," applied to the pairs in the game of *k'ap t'ái shap*, p. 513, are the same as those used to designate the broken and undivided lines in the *Yik King*, and that

---

*Report of the Proceedings of the Numismatic and Antiquarian Society of Philadelphia, 1890-91, p. 65.

†Buddhism in Thibet, London, 1863, p. 315.

‡Col. W. W. Rockhill informs me that he never saw dice used in Thibet except for fortune telling. According to Col. Rockhill, the Thibetan name for dice is *sho*, and a person who throws dice, *mojyab ken*. He tells me that he always saw four dice used in Thibet and North China. These dice have no "six." There is a picture of the god *Pal-dan-hlamo* holding a bag of dominoes or dice in the superb Thibetan collection deposited by him in the U. S. National Museum.

the diagram (fig. 33)* which is given by Legge † as the accepted form of the *Lok Shü*, or "Lo writing," which is referred to in the *Yik King* as one of the sources of inspiration for its broken and undivided lines,‡ is composed of light and dark circles similar to the domino dots.

I may suggest, in conclusion, that dominoes may have been first used as counters or tallies in a dice game or in a method of fortune telling with dice. They existed in their present form in China in the year 1120 A. D., according to the Chinese records, with similar astrological associations as at the present day. They are clearly descended from dice, and particularly from that game with two dice which appears to have been introduced into China from western Asia.

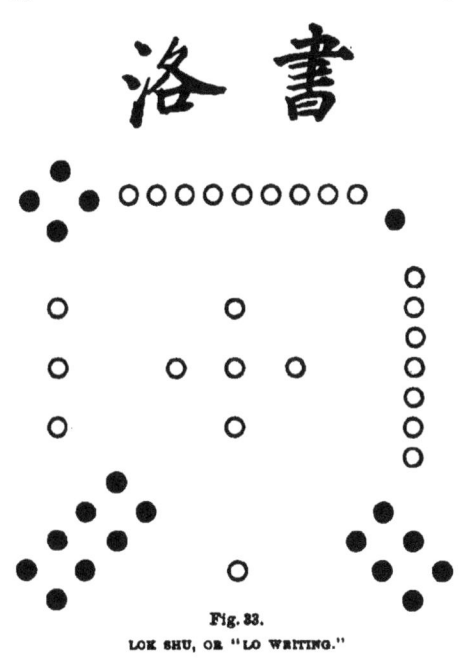

Fig. 33.
LOK SHU, OR "LO WRITING."

---

* This diagram coincides with the most renowned of the arithmetical squares which are used as charms both by Hindus and Mohammedans in India. It is usually written as below, an inversion of the Chinese arrangement.

```
6 1 8
7 5 3
2 9 4
```

This square appears in its numerical form on the Thibetan charts, reproduced by Schlagintweit, where it is arranged in the Chinese order.

It is believed in India, said one of my Mohammedan informants, that to write this charm will bring good luck and money by honest means. The object for which it is used is always written beneath it. He told me that his grandfather wrote it every day after prayers and would place beneath it the words *ruk*, "bread," or *chardj*, "expenses." Such numbered diagrams are cut in squares, each containing a number. These are made into pills with wheaten bread and thrown into a pond or river to be eaten by fish.

Another Indian, a Hindu, says that this magic square is called in Hindustani *Pundra no yuntra*, or the "15 yuntra."

It is written both with numerals and with dots. In the latter case the set of dots from 1 to 9 frequently are made each of a different color and certain names are given to them.

It is not improbable that this diagram was borrowed by the Chinese from India, and that, too, at a much later period than is usually assigned to it by the Chinese. The writer found a copy of it—in Arabic numerals, among the written charms in a soldier's kit captured in Tonquin—in the Municipal Museum of the city of Havre.

The spots, like those on the dice, are doubtless survivals of a primitive system of notation, like that which existed in Mexico at the time of the Conquest.

† Legge, Rev. Dr. James, The Yê King, Oxford, 1882. Introduction, p. 18.
‡ *Ibid.*, Appendix III, Sec. I, par. 73.

This book is a preservation photocopy.
It is made in compliance with copyright law
and produced on acid-free archival
60# book weight paper
which meets the requirements of
ANSI/NISO Z39.48-1992 (permanence of paper)

Preservation photocopying and binding
by
Acme Bookbinding
Charlestown, Massachusetts

2002

Lightning Source UK Ltd.
Milton Keynes UK
UKHW030747210219
337759UK00006B/723/P